KÖNIGS ERLÄUTERUNGEN SPEZIAL

W0328799

Textanalyse und Interpretation zu

F. Scott Fitzgerald

THE GREAT GATSBY

Patrick Charles

Alle erforderlichen Infos für Abitur, Matura, Klausur und Referat
plus Musteraufgaben mit Lösungsansätzen

Bange Verlag

Zitierte Ausgabe:
Fitzgerald, F. Scott: *The Great Gatsby*, ed. Susanne Lenz. Stuttgart: Reclam, 1995 (Reclams Universal Bibliothek Nr. 9242).

Über den Autor dieser Erläuterung:
Patrick Charles wurde 1973 in Bournemouth, Südengland geboren und studierte englische Literatur an der Universität von Newcastle. 1993 zog er nach Berlin, wo er eine Ausbildung zum Buchhändler machte und zehn Jahre lang als Buchhändler arbeitete. Seit 2004 ist er als freiberuflicher Autor von Schulbüchern und Lernhilfen und als Übersetzer im Kulturbereich tätig. Er lebt mit seiner Familie in Berlin.

Das Werk und seine Teile sind urheberrechtlich geschützt. Jede Verwertung in anderen als den gesetzlich zugelassenen Fällen bedarf der vorherigen schriftlichen Einwilligung des Verlages.
Hinweis zu § 52 a UrhG: Die öffentliche Zugänglichmachung eines für den Unterrichtsgebrauch an Schulen bestimmten Werkes ist stets nur mit Einwilligung des Berechtigten zulässig.

3. Auflage 2016
ISBN: 978-3-8044-3122-5
PDF: 978-3-8044-5122-3, EPUB: 978-3-8044-4122-4
© 2013 by Bange Verlag GmbH, 96142 Hollfeld
Alle Rechte vorbehalten!
Titelbild: Filmposter *The Great Gatsby* (TV-Film, UK/USA 2000).
Darsteller: Mira Sorvino, Toby Stephens © Cinetext/Sammlung Richter
Druck und Weiterverarbeitung: Tiskárna Akcent, Vimperk

1. AT A GLANCE – THE MOST IMPORTANT POINTS

In order for readers to be able to find the most relevant sections quickly and easily, here is a summary and overview of the following book:

Part 2 is an introduction to the author and his works and the contemporary world.

⇨ p. 11 ff.
→ F. Scott Fitzgerald lived 1896–1940 and was considered the chronicler of the Jazz Age.

⇨ p. 14 ff.
→ The 1920s were a period of rapid and profound changes in American society, industry, culture and commercial life.

⇨ p. 26 ff.
→ He wrote novels and short stories about the society around him: his main themes included the promise of youth and the despair of age, and love and wealth.

Part 3 offers analyses and interpretations of various elements of the novel.

The Great Gatsby – Origins and Sources

⇨ p. 33 ff.
→ The book was published in 1925.
→ It was inspired in part by time the Fitzgeralds spent living on Long Island.
→ The book picked up on themes which Fitzgerald had been writing about in his earlier novels and stories.
→ During the writing process Fitzgerald knew that *The Great Gatsby* would be his most important work.

Summaries

➪ p. 38 ff.

The novel is set on Long Island, New York, and tells the story, narrated by Nick Carraway, of mysterious millionaire Jay Gatsby and his love for Daisy Buchanan. Gatsby and Daisy had been in love before the First World War. During the war they lost contact and Daisy married Tom, a wealthy and brutal womaniser. As Nick discovers during the summer of 1922, Gatsby came from poor origins and changed his identity as a boy. He became wealthy in order to become worthy of Daisy. When the two of them are reunited and begin an affair, Gatsby and Tom confront each other. Daisy chooses Tom. Daisy accidentally kills Tom's mistress Myrtle in a motor accident and Myrtle's husband takes revenge by killing Gatsby, whom Tom has told him is responsible. At the end of the novel Tom and Daisy have disappeared and Nick organises Gatsby's lonely funeral before returning to his home in the Midwest, shocked and disappointed by all he has witnessed.

Structure

➪ p. 59 ff.

The novel is narrated two years after the events by one of the characters, and therefore has an unusually complex narrative structure. Readers are encouraged to assess the events and the characters from different perspectives. This structure allows the author to use various voices and viewpoints in telling the story. Fitzgerald, writing "through" Nick, is able to give the novel a circular framework. Nick's distanced yet participatory role in the novel also complicates the structure, as there is no clear centre, and the roles of the characters within the novel are subject to interpretation.

Characters – Constellations and Characteristics

The main characters:

⇨ p. 69 ff.

Nick Carraway

the narrator: distant cousin to Daisy, familiar with Tom from their time in college, romantically involved with Jordan, and by the end of the novel Gatsby's only friend. Nick witnesses Gatsby and Daisy's reunion and the tragedies that follow, with the deaths of Gatsby, Myrtle and George. He returns to the Midwest, disturbed by the world of the East.

⇨ p. 71 ff.

Jay Gatsby

born James Gatz, he tried to escape his poor origins by becoming Jay Gatsby. He learned how to be rich from Dan Cody, fell in love with Daisy after enlisting to serve in World War I, and when he returned became wealthy distributing illegal alcohol across the country. He wins Daisy briefly but she returns to Tom, and Gatsby is then killed by George Wilson in a case of mistaken identity.

⇨ p. 75 ff.

Daisy Buchanan

beautiful and wealthy, Daisy was in love with Gatsby before the war, but was unwilling or unable to wait for him and married Tom Buchanan. She accidentally kills Myrtle Wilson while driving Gatsby's car.

⇨ p. 78 ff.

Tom Buchanan

an arrogant, wealthy, brutish bigot, Tom is having an affair with Myrtle Wilson. When Gatsby challenges him for Daisy, Tom persuades her to stay with him because they share a bond which Gatsby, coming from the lower classes, can never understand. He directs the vengeful George towards Gatsby.

Jordan Baker

⇨ p. 81 f.

a friend of Daisy and Tom, and Nick's lover. Jordan is a cool, modern woman, a professional golfer, and fundamentally dishonest.

Myrtle Wilson

⇨ p. 82 f.

frustrated and lonely, Myrtle is having an affair with Tom. She is killed by Daisy driving Gatsby's car.

George Wilson

⇨ p. 84 f.

runs a garage in an industrial wasteland. He is exhausted and poor and longs to escape to a better life in the West. After Myrtle is killed he takes revenge by killing Gatsby and then commits suicide.

Other characters:

⇨ p. 85 ff.

Henry Gatz – James Gatz's father
Dan Cody – The wealthy adventurer who inspired James Gatz to become Jay Gatsby
Meyer Wolfshiem – A gambler in New York who helped Gatsby establish his illegal business
"Owl Eyes" – A man who attends Gatsby's parties and funeral
Michaelis – A friend of George Wilson
Catherine – Myrtle's sister

Notes on Themes

Here are notes on the major themes in the novel with quotations and brief analyses:

⇨ p. 91 ff.

→ America and the American Dream
→ Society and wealth
→ The Jazz Age: the modern world
→ Desire and the past
→ Vision

Style and Language

➪ p. 115 ff.

Fitzgerald has always been praised as a writer whose language is unusually rich and evocative. In *The Great Gatsby* he makes excellent use of diverse "voices" and tones, as well as intricate imagery, to enhance and deepen the ideas he is expressing.

→ Seasons and other imagery and symbolism
→ Ambiguity
→ Colour symbolism
→ Narrative tone

Approaches to Interpretation

➪ p. 126 ff.

Here is a brief look at three major themes focussed on by literary studies on *The Great Gatsby*.

→ Gender roles
→ American identity and the myths of The Frontier
→ The modern world

2. F. SCOTT FITZGERALD: LIFE & WORKS

2.1 Biography

F. Scott Fitzgerald (1896–1940) © ullstein bild – Röhnert

YEAR	PLACE	EVENT	AGE
Sep. 24, 1896	Saint Paul, Minnesota (USA)	Born	
1908–11	St Paul Academy, Saint Paul Minnesota	Student at St Paul Academy.	12–15
1909-11	Newman School, Hackensack New Jersey	First publication: short story *The Mystery of the Raymond Mortgage* published in the school magazine.	13–15
1911-13	Princeton University, Princeton New Jersey	Attended Catholic prep school (to prepare students for university), and continued to write short stories – three are published in the school magazine – and stage plays, two of which are staged at school.	15–17
1913–17	Kansas, Kentucky, Georgia, Alabama and Long Island	Began studying but dropped out in 1917. During his time at Princeton he met future literary figures like Edmund Wilson, and had more stories published in the university magazine.	17–21
1917–19	New York, Saint Paul	Military service. Joined the army after quitting university and was stationed at various army bases around the country. Met and fell in love with Zelda. First novel, *The Romantic Egotist*, was rejected by the publisher Scribners.	21–23

2.1 Biography

YEAR	PLACE	EVENT	AGE
1919–20	Europe, Saint Paul, Long Island	Discharged from the army, worked for an advertising agency in New York: continued to write and publish short stories. Engagement to Zelda was broken off, but they eventually married in April 1920. First indications of serious alcohol problem. Returning to St Paul, rewrote the novel *This Side of Paradise*, later published by Scribners (March 1920): this was followed by his first collection of stories (*Flappers and Philosophers*) in Sept. 1920.	23–24
1921–25	Europe, Hollywood	Scott and Zelda's first trip to Europe was followed by publication of the novel *The Beautiful and the Damned*. Daughter Frances born Oct. 1921. The major novella *The Diamond as Big as the Ritz* published in June 1922. More stories and another collection published. They continued to travel in Europe. Themes and ideas for *The Great Gatsby* were forming during this period. The novel was written in France and completed and revised in Rome. *Gatsby* was published by Scribners in April 1925.	25–29
1925–30	Europe, America, North Africa	European travels continued, especially Paris and the French Riviera: Scott became friendly with Ernest Hemingway and other American writers living in Paris. Recurring alcohol problems affected his health. Zelda suffered a nervous breakdown and was hospitalised in Switzerland: she would be in and out of hospitals for the rest of her life. Scott continued to write and publish stories.	29–34

YEAR	PLACE	EVENT	AGE
1931–1940	Hollywood	During the final years of his life Scott wrote two more novels and several short stories. His increasing debts forced him to work freelance in Hollywood. His alcoholism worsened, and he eventually died of a heart attack in Hollywood on 21 December 1940, aged 44. Zelda died in a fire in a hospital eight years later.	35–44

2.2 Contemporary Background

The Great Gatsby was written during the years in which the 20th century really began. The old world had died in the First World War, and a new one was being shaped: by the energy and freedom of free market capitalism, rapidly increasing populations and by the breakdown of traditional hierarchies – the Jazz Age.

The political and social situation

The Great Gatsby was written during the years in which the 20th century really began. The old world had died in the First World War[1], and a new one was being shaped: by the energy and freedom of free market capitalism, rapidly increasing populations and great leaps forward in technology and in the availability and quantity of consumer goods; and by **the energy and freedom released by the breakdown of traditional hierarchies** and the emergence of a hedonist, youth-oriented "pop culture" centred on jazz music, parties and sexual liberation. Fitzgerald defined this energy in his 1931 essay *Echoes of the Jazz Age* as "all the nervous energy stored up and unexpended in the War"[2]. This energy was spent on hedonism rather than social activism. As he wrote in 1931, "the events of 1919 left us cynical rather than revolutionary [...] It was characteristic of the Jazz Age that it had no interest in politics at all."[3]

---

1 1914–18: The USA became active in 1917 when Germany began attacking ships in the Atlantic.
2 http://fitzgerald.narod.ru/crackup/056e-eho.htm
3 ibid.

The Jazz Age

Fitzgerald invented the term The Jazz Age, which was also called **the Golden 20s** (usually referring to Europe) or the Roaring 20s, and was characterised by an equally powerful dark side, a sense of loss, emptiness and disorientation for a "lost generation" surrounded by the decay of traditional social structures and memories of the unprecedented slaughter of the First World War. Sandwiched between the War to End All Wars and the Great Depression[4], this period is a fascinating and evocative period in American history and set the scene for many lasting myths of American identity and culture.

Politics and the economy

Isolationism and economic growth

Coming out of the First World War, the United States was led by Woodrow Wilson (President 1913–1921), a progressive[5] who remains controversial to this day. While **he initiated many important reforms, including laws restricting child labour and regulating work conditions**, he proved to be deeply racist in both his personal views and political dealing. He had been in favour of the US joining the League of Nations, an international organisation of nations formed after the peace treaties at the end of the First World War, but was defeated by the Senate. He was succeeded as president by Warren G. Harding, a conservative isolationist who rejected the progressive era's attempts to reform government and force social change. The US became increasingly inward-looking from this point on. As well as this international attitude of refusing to "join the club", taxes on imported goods were raised (encouraging domestic consumers to buy American goods) and there

---

4 A worldwide economic recession which began with the Wall Street stock market crash of October 29 1929 and lasted until 1941.

5 American progessivism was a political movement lasting from 1890 until 1930 which attempt to fight corruption in politics and promote social and economic reforms.

was an end to free immigration. Harding was followed by Calvin Coolidge, who was president when the Great Depression began in 1929, and who continued to raise taxes on imports and cut federal taxes. These three Republican presidents worked to strengthen the relationship between government and big businesses in the US.

Mass media: press, radio, cinema newsreels

The war years had been dominated by emotional, patriotic political activity: following the war there was a return to what President Harding called "normalcy" – basically, to the ideal of a peaceful and productive United States. He used the new mass media – the press, radio, and cinema newsreels – to promote his vision in a "front porch campaign"[6], capturing the public imagination as he was featured in the press welcoming film stars and celebrities from the world of sport, entertainment and industry to his home in Ohio.

The "return to normalcy" proved difficult, however, as the period following the First World War was dominated by **massive industrial, commercial and social growth** and consequent shifts in lifestyle and culture. It was indeed a time of great prosperity with so many men from the armed forces returning to join the workforce, but Harding's "normalcy" was an idealised myth, and the new reality was very different.

Prohibition, racism and immigration

The isolationism and provincialism of the US during this era can be seen in many areas. Efforts to encourage consumption of domestic products are an obvious point, as are the increasingly restrictive immigration laws. These were accompanied by other phenomena such as Prohibition and the revival of the Ku Klux Klan, the white supremacist secret society based in the American South.

---

6 Political campaigns in which the candidate stays at or near home and supporters are encouraged to come and listen to speeches.

In 1919 laws were passed which prohibited the manufacture, transport and sale of alcohol. These laws were demanded by a powerful movement which believed that alcohol was responsible for widespread criminality and immorality. Ironically, one immediate result of Prohibition was to create an unprecedented source of income and field of activity for domestic organised crime. The Prohibitionists had not realised that the American appetite for alcohol was so strong: illegal nightclubs ("speakeasies") sprung up like mushrooms all over the country. Alcohol was smuggled in from Canada and produced in secret in the US, and **bootlegging – the illegal distribution and sale of alcohol** – was largely controlled by gangsters, most famously Al Capone. The enormous profits to be made led to the establishment of the Italian-American Mafia (Cosa Nostra) as a powerful and permanent fixture in American life.

The ban on alcohol contributed to the wealth of organised crime and caused widespread corruption

Organised crime in North America, as in most Western cultures, is largely the business of immigrants. Discrimination in many areas led generations of Irish, Italians, Chinese, Russians, Armenians and other nationalities to form groups to protect their neighbourhoods and interests, which has often given rise to gangs and organisations more interested in servicing illegal markets – prostitution, gambling, drugs – and using violence to keep control.

Immigration is a major factor in the history of the United States. It is, like Australia, a nation of immigrants. The dominant culture has, throughout its history, reacted to immigration and immigrants in different ways. Before the period relevant to *The Great Gatsby*, the attitude was much more open: and then the Immigration Act of 1924 defined strict limits to the number of immigrants from particular countries who were allowed to enter the US each year. This Act itself replaced the 1921 Emergency Quota Act, which was designed to restrict the numbers of immigrants from Eastern Europe, the Middle East, Asia and India. The goal shared by both

Many white Americans tried to protect what they saw as their cultural identity against immigrants

Acts was the protection of the ideal of "American homogeneity" (which is rooted in white Western European cultures). This racist law-making from the government was mirrored in the revival of violent nativist groups, who demanded preferential treatment for "natives" (the descendants of white Europeans) and the defence of their cultural values, and who were hostile to immigrants. The segregation of blacks and whites throughout the country was accompanied by the emergence of immigrant ghettoes in urban areas.

Consumers

Industrial and commercial innovations caused great changes in society

The rapid development of industrial production and the innovations made possible by electricity completely changed the economic make-up of the country. Rural sectors like farming and mining suffered, but the cities grew, and there were more products that more people wanted to have – most importantly, automobiles. Everyone wanted a car. The manufacturing industry became increasingly important, and led to a boom in construction. Roads, highways, bridges, tunnels had to be built, improved and maintained. **This meant work – and more work meant more money**, which led in turn to more people buying more products. The US economy, much more so than that of the European nations, was focussed on mass production and consumerism.

Automobile industry

Cars had been a luxury before the war. This had changed by the 1920s – mass production has seldom been as evident as it was in the US automobile industry[7]. In 1912 roughly 187,380 cars had been produced in America. By 1922 this figure had risen to 1.862,290 – an almost tenfold increase. More than 15 million

---

7 Born in 1890, the automobile became a powerful symbol for American society and above all industry. The US car industry was literally the motor of the nation's economy for decades. By the end of the 1920s the industry was dominated by three companies: Ford, General Motors and Chrysler.

Model Ts, the first affordable, mass produced car, had been sold by the time they were discontinued in 1927.

The increased ownership of cars created a raft of new service industries, from road building to garages, repairmen, used car salesmen, motels and filling stations. Architects were needed to build garages in which people could house their shiny new automobiles. **Everyone wanted a car, and cars completely changed lifestyles and society in the US**.

Radio

Another major innovation was radio – not only as a source of entertainment, making possible such phenomena as soap operas and popular music, but also as a channel for mass marketing. For the first time in history it was possible for manufacturers to advertise their products nation-wide. This meant that there was a vast range of products, services and ideas now available to all Americans – mass culture was born, the culture which has come to dominate capitalist societies. This is the culture of consumerism, entertainment, and individualism.

Culture

Two important innovations are of special relevance to this era – automobiles and jazz music. Both promised freedom, and represented something that was, above all, new. **Anything seemed possible** – the old world was gone, the traditions had been broken, the terrible threat of the war was gone and the spirit of modernity was dominant. Automobiles allowed individuals to travel wherever they wanted, whenever they wanted. Freedom and independence were offered by this new commodity which was also a powerful status symbol.

Jazz music

Jazz was the music of the African-Americans: growing from the blues, ragtime, and the raucous lively stomp of the New Orleans Dixie bands, by the 1920s jazz had become a respected art form,

Short hair, short skirt, smoking: Drawing by an illustration of a flapper by John Held, 1925. © ullstein bild – The Granger Collection

largely thanks to Duke Ellington[8], and was producing virtuoso musicians like **trumpeter Louis Armstrong, vocalist Bessie Smith and pianist Earl Hines**. Jazz was a radical departure from the popular music that had existed up until the 20th century: it was free, wild, exciting, and it reflected human concerns and contradictions in an unprecedented manner. Many white Americans were fascinated by jazz, and the thrilling, decadent sound – associated with **hot nightclubs and wild parties** – became increasingly popular. Jazz was a cultural phenomenon beyond its importance as a musical genre, as it was the vehicle for the integration of African-American creativity, traditions and ideals into the predominantly white middle-class culture in the USA.

Along with jazz came dancing. There were **waves of fashionable new dances** throughout the 1920s – foxtrot, swing, Charleston – which popularised a hedonist, free-living culture of jazz-listening, anti-Prohibition rebellion. And the Flappers were at the forefront of this new craze.

Flappers

Flappers were rebels – young women who wore short skirts and short hair, who drank, drove cars, danced to jazz bands, attended casual sex "petting parties" and generally did all they could to show how little they cared for traditional authority and patterns of behaviour and morality.

8 1899–1974 Jazz composer, pianist and band leader who preferred the term "American music".

The word was originally an English term which had become progressively milder – in the 17th century is was used for prostitutes, and by the 19th century it meant a lively young girl – and by 1920 it had become a widely used label for impetuous, irresponsible young women who were more **interested in fashions, dances and men with cars than with politics** and correct behaviour. Flappers pushed at the limits of sexual restrictions and morality, and their behaviour challenged existing ideas of gender roles. Women had won the right to vote in the US in 1920 after a long struggle, but were still held back in society and in the workplace. Dominant religious and moral opinion held that women should be sober, modest and obedient. The flappers were anything but that.

Impetuous, irresponsible young women

Through the work of popular illustrators and films like *The Flapper*, as well as through fiction, including stories by Fitzgerald (who referred to his wife Zelda as the "first American flapper"), the flapper had become a **symbol of independent young women** whose need for personal freedom and satisfaction outweighed their duty to marry and have children. Like most aggressively modern youth movements, flappers developed their own slang, their own dress codes, dance styles, and were eventually assimilated into the mainstream of society. Flapper fashion – the slim, boyish body, French-inspired couture and the daring use of make-up – was toned down and assimilated, in the same way as much of what was considered "flapper behaviour" – the smoking, drinking and jazz dancing – gradually became less shocking. **The flappers' disregard for convention** was one aspect of a generation of women who saw it as their right to have fun how and when they wanted and, beyond that, to live their lives on their own terms: financially independent and self-determined. Although flapper culture vanished swiftly with the onset of the Great Depression, the radical changes it brought to women's lifestyles and identities was to have a lasting effect in American society.

The rising popularity of jazz was greatly helped by the radio. The first mass medium, radio enabled both the spread of mass culture across the country and the introduction of mass marketing techniques to support and constantly feed a growing consumerist culture. Radio initiated the celebrity focus which has come to dominate Western culture: individual athletes became superstars: singers and performers, actors and radio personalities, could now be made famous far beyond the reach of concert halls and theatres. There was a broad range of programmes on the radio stations across the United States: as is often the case with pioneer stages in the development of a new technology or medium, there was a lot of experimentation, innovation and creative exploration.

The world of sport

The world of sport was also fundamentally changed during this period. As sportsmen and women became superstars and radio created a new breed of sports journalism, the perception of sports themselves changed. What had been niche sports, limited to the upper classes, were now more accessible – **a prime example here is golf**, also relevant to *The Great Gatsby*, a sport which had long been the exclusive pastime of the wealthy elite.

The broadening appeal of sports as a spectator event contributed to the idea of a new kind of heroism. Rather than being an activity in which men could prove their masculinity in competition with others, sports was now a world in which heroic efforts could be immediately mythologised by journalists and vast crowds. The most famous example of this celebrity-hero sports figure is the baseball player Babe Ruth.

The new sporting heroes were mirrored by new stars of the movies and the music world – and even criminals could attract adulation. In earlier years, heroes were typically those who had endured great hardship or fantastic adventures to advance their country or religion, in military campaigns or exploration. Now the emerging stars, men and women who embodied the spirit of the age, included aviator Charles Lindbergh, cinema idols Rudolph Valentino and Charlie Chaplin, musicians Duke Ellington and Louis Armstrong, dancer Josephine Baker and even gangster Al Capone. This celebrity culture was new at the time, and has continued to grow ever since.

The literary context

The Lost Generation

Fitzgerald, Hemingway, John Dos Passos

The Great Gatsby is the epitome of the Jazz Age in literature. More than any other book **it examines the atmosphere and mechanics and desires of the era**. It was of course not the only book to do so, and it was also not Fitzgerald's first work. He had been writing about the world he knew – the world of love, wealth, status and lack of orientation in young urban society – in short stories and novels. He had also got to know many other writers and artists of his generation, most importantly, perhaps, Ernest Hemingway[9], with whom he had spent time in his travels to Europe. Hemingway's novel *The Sun Also Rises* (1926) looks at the lack of direction and sense of loss felt by the so-called "Lost Generation"[10] who came of age during the First World War. Fitzgerald also greatly respected the work of his friend John Dos Passos. Although Dos Passos was more experimental as a writer and more explicitly political, his classic novel *Manhattan Transfer* (1925) also proved

---

9 1899–1961 American novelist and Nobel Prize Laureate, who spent years living in Paris and was famous for his robustly masculine personality and his literary themes: love, war and loss.

10 The term was coined by Gertrude Stein and first used in print by Hemingway in 1926. It refers to the generation who grew up during WWI. In literature, it is concerned with themes of alienation and the lack of orientation in the post-war world.

extremely perceptive in its understanding of the implications of mass production and mass culture which had been unleashed in the USA.

William Faulkner, T.S. Eliot

Other writers who were active at the time include Nobel prize-winning novelist William Faulkner, so closely associated with the American South; Chicago poet Carl Sandburg: T.S. Eliot, author of *The Waste Land* (1922), one of the most influential works of Western literature, whose use of the legends of the Holy Grail also left their mark on *Gatsby*: and Sherwood Anderson, whose *Winesburg, Ohio* (1919) pre-empted the Modernist concern with emptiness and isolation.

Zelda Fitzgerald

Fitzgerald's wife Zelda also wrote, and although for a long time she was not taken seriously as a writer and dismissed as a famous fashion icon and celebrity socialite whose novel was largely autobiographical**, she has in recent years been re-evaluated** as a much more substantial artist in her own right. The importance of her novel *Save Me the Waltz* (1932) is now acknowledged for its examination of the stresses to which women were subjected during the period, as well as being a fascinating twin to her husband's *Tender is the Night* (1934), which also dealt with the failure of their marriage.

Modernism

Reactions to the industrial, commercial world of the 20th century

The 1920s was the era in which Modernism swept through the arts, from architecture to sculpture, manifesting in countless movements from Cubism to Futurism, Bauhaus, the Dadaists and the Surrealists. Generally speaking, **Modernism rejects traditional certainties** (such as unalterable truths or the idea of a benevolent God) in trying to find new answers to contemporary issues, and was very concerned with form. In literature Modernists included, as well as the Lost Generation writers, the British Bloomsbury

Set (including Virginia Woolf and E.M. Forster): Gertrude Stein, a feminist pioneer; Marcel Proust, author of a 7-volume novel which inspired many Modernist writers in its fusion of shifting levels of location, time and consciousness; and Bertolt Brecht, who revolutionised and modernised theatre and the roles of spectator and performer/artist. Despite the thematic and formal diversity of these writers and their works, they all confronted the same fundamental issues: **life in the aftermath of the First World War**, in a world increasingly dominated by commercialised, urbanised, industrialised culture. Whether this new world with its mechanical, aggressive energies was embraced – as it was by the Futurists, for example – or approached more cautiously, with sadness, irony or disgust, it had an undeniable influence on the content and the nature of what was being written and created.

2.3 Notes on Other Important Works

Francis Scott Fitzgerald wrote four novels (a fifth was published posthumously) and dozens of short stories. He also published essays and worked on screenplays. Fitzgerald's major work was concerned with people, places and situations with which he was familiar – the East Coast, the aimlessness of young men, love, status, wealth and greed, and the lifestyles of the Jazz Age.

Francis Scott Fitzgerald wrote four novels (a fifth was published posthumously) and dozens of short stories, which varied widely in quality from substantial pieces like *The Diamond as Big as The Ritz* (1922) to lightweight tales produced when money ran short. He also published essays and worked on screenplays while he was living in Hollywood. He adapted one of his short stories (*The Vegetable*, 1923) into a play. Fitzgerald's major work was concerned with people, places and situations with which he was familiar – the East Coast, the aimlessness of young men, love, status, wealth and greed, and the lifestyles of Jazz Age. Here is a brief introduction to other relevant works which had a direct thematic relevance to the ideas he would cover in *The Great Gatsby*.

The novels

PUBLICATION DATE	TITLE
1920	*This Side of Paradise*
1922	*The Beautiful and the Damned*
1925	*The Great Gatsby*
1934	*Tender is the Night*
1941 (posthumous)	*The Love of the Last Tycoon*

This Side of Paradise

Popular and successful

Fitzgerald's début novel reworked his earlier, unpublished attempt, *The Romantic Egotist*. As with most of his work it is autobiographically influenced: Fitzgerald was a writer who wrote about what he knew. The book follows Amory Blaine. Convinced of his shining future, he goes to Princeton, and later serves during the First World War, before failing to marry a wealthy young woman in New York. Having disappointed his own expectations, by the end of the novel Amory is 24, alone, and forced to accept that his own egotistical nature has denied him happiness. The **themes of greed, status and love**, which would always interest Fitzgerald as a writer, are evident here. *Paradise* was a great success and while it did not make him rich, the fame and respect it brought him did allow Fitzgerald to convince Zelda to marry him, and to earn more money for his short stories.

The Beautiful and the Damned

Least admired of his novels

Again borrowing from Fitzgerald's experience (most tragically in the central character's alcoholism), this least popular of his novels follows the physical and spiritual decline of Anthony Patch and his wife Gloria. Anthony has one goal: to inherit his grandfather's wealth. The emptiness of this life feeds his alcoholism, and the novel mercilessly portrays the bitterness and decay of the Patches. Fitzgerald's **second novel was not as commercially successful as his début**, and has often been judged his least successful by critics, despite its unusually uncompromising examination of the lack of direction and values that afflicted the Lost Generation.

Tender is the Night

Most personal of the novels

Like *Gatsby*, his fourth novel was a critical and commercial disappointment when it was published, but has since been acknowledged as a major work. This is again a **deeply autobiographical work**, making use of the troubles in Scott's marriage to Zelda, her mental illness and hospitalisation, their lifestyle, and even his own father's death. The novel tells the story of Dick Diver, a young American psychiatrist who falls in love with the beautiful and unstable Nicole. Their marriage is doomed by their imbalance – Nicole is a patient, beautiful, ill and needy: Dick, her doctor, is young, free, strong and brilliant. As Dick and Nicole struggle through affairs and jealousies and resentment, he comes to feel that the burden of caring for her has ruined any chance he had of fulfilling the brilliant potential of his youth. The novel ends with Nicole having left him for another man, and Dick living and working in obscurity in New York State.

It was a struggle for Fitzgerald to write this novel. He had begun an early version immediately after finishing *Gatsby*, in 1925, and continued to work at it until its completion in 1933. **This last novel**

to have been published during his lifetime seems to have been the most intensely personal of all his works.

The Love of the Last Tycoon

Published after his death

Originally begun as *The Last Tycoon*, this unfinished novel about a Hollywood producer was published in 1941. Fitzgerald's relationship with Hollywood was not good. He had worked for the studios in 1927, and again in 1931 and 1932. He despised the work he did there – which was entirely for money, with no artistic ambition on his part – and seems to have been unpopular with his employers, as well. In 1937 he was fired by the famous Metro-Goldwyn-Mayer studio for drinking. *The Last Tycoon* is believed to be a "roman a clef" – a novel about a real person concealed behind a screen of fiction – based on Hollywood producer Irving Thalberg.

Short story collections

PUBLICATION DATE	TITLE
1921	*Flappers and Philosophers*
1922	*Tales of the Jazz Age*
1926	*All the Sad Young Men*
1935	*Taps at Reveille*

Flappers and Philosophers

These stories made his reputation as the chronicler of the Jazz Age

His first collection included *Head and Shoulders* (written and published in 1920), the story of the relationship between the intellectual Horace and the dancer Marcia and the eventual reversal of their roles (the "shoulders" support the "head"). This story was about unequal relationships – a major theme in much of his work, especially in *The Great Gatsby* and *Tender is the Night* – and the problems of combining creative ambition with romantic relationships, a theme he confronted in his own life, dealing with Zelda's mental health issues.

Bernice Bobs Her Hair is another famous story from this collection, originally published in 1920, about a bright young girl who is taught how to make herself popular with boys, providing a glimpse into the young urban lifestyle of the period.

Tales of the Jazz Age

Includes important piece *May Day*

The lengthy story (it could be considered a novella) *May Day* is important, as it looks at the dark side of the Jazz Age, and tackles two of his major themes: lost and aimless youth, and the wealth and society of New York. The events which inspired the story were the riots in New York on May 1 1919 and the police brutality – which he described in the essay *Echoes of the Jazz Age* as "the sort of measure bound to alienate the more intelligent young men from the prevailing order"[11], and characterised as "tyranny". Other notable stories in this collection include the fantasy tales *The Curious Case of Benjamin Button*, which was made into a film in 2008, and *The Diamond as Big as The Ritz*.

All the Sad Young Men

Stories exploring the plot and themes he was to use in *The Great Gatsby*

This collection includes stories written during or just after the writing of *The Great Gatsby*. It includes *The Rich Boy*, which examines the effects wealth can have on a person, and which was considered by Fitzgerald himself, as well as many critics, to be among his very best work. Another story in this collection which can be thematically grouped with *The Great Gatsby* is *Winter Dreams*. This story is about an ambitious, strong-willed poor boy who is desperately in

---

11 http://fitzgerald.narod.ru/crackup/056e-eho.htm

love with a selfish girl from a wealthier background, and who becomes amazingly wealthy. He later discovers that the object of his affections has married a cruel man and become a faded housewife. The similarities to the plot and characters of *The Great Gatsby* are inescapable.

Taps at Reveille

This final collection of his stories to be published in his lifetime was also the largest. It included *Babylon Revisited*, which is set in 1929, after the stock market crash which triggered the Great Depression, and can be seen as Fitzgerald's farewell to the decade he had helped identify and define in his fiction.

Melancholy stories saying goodbye to the Roaring 20s

Essay

PUBLICATION DATE	TITLE
1931	*Echoes of the Jazz Age*

This essay was Fitzgerald‘s requiem and official farewell to the age which he named and with which his work – and his celebrity life with Zelda – was so closely connected. In this short text **he defines the characteristics of the age** ("it was an age of miracles, it was an age of art, it was an age of excess, and it was an age of satire"[12]) and looks back on various factors which defined it. These include fashion, language, the "private mobility" that cars suddenly made possible and the increasingly liberated sexuality. His opinion, looking back, is that the generation of the Jazz Age "overreached itself less through lack of morals than through lack of taste". The general tone of the essay is one of bitterness and nostalgia: bitterness,

———

12 http://fitzgerald.narod.ru/crackup/056e-eho.htm

perhaps, for the missed opportunities to have used the "nervous energy stored up and unexpended in the War" for something more productive and socially progressive than hedonism, and nostalgia for the intense feelings and excitement of his own youth.

3. ANALYSES AND INTERPRETATIONS

3.1 Origins and Sources

The story and themes of *The Great Gatsby* – doomed love, wealth and status, the social life of the East Coast – had been tackled by Fitzgerald before. The plot appeared in an early form in the short story *Winter Dream* (1922), and the themes were present in many of his earlier stories and his two previous novels. The initial idea for the book had come to him as early as 1922 (the year in which the book is set), after spending time living on Long Island, where the novel is also set. It was only after moving to France in 1924 that he began to work seriously on the novel, the importance of which he realised early. He saw it as the chance for him to prove himself as a real writer of literature, rather than a professional producer of short stories for magazines. He finished work on the novel in 1925, and it was published by Scribner's of New York in April that year.

Origin and inspiration

Inspired by Long Island

From 1922 to 1923 F. Scott Fitzgerald, his wife Zelda and their daughter Scottie lived in a rented house in Great Neck, Long Island. This became the West Egg of the book – East Egg is based on Sands Point, across the water in Port Washington. The **Fitzgeralds were at this time a celebrity couple**, famous for their youth, beauty and modern lifestyle. In the early '20s, Long Island was popular with other modern celebrities, and was associated with "new money" – this distinction between "old" and "new" money was highlighted in the fictional West and East Egg communities in *The Great Gatsby*. Many of the features with which the Roaring 20s and the Jazz Age were associated were concentrated in this environment: the wild lifestyles of the wealthy and the new freedoms offered by cars, music and dancing shattered traditional expectations. Fitzgerald incorporated these changes in the book he was planning.

Composition and writing

The book was important to Fitzgerald and he worked hard and long on it

Fitzgerald seems to have had **difficulties in arranging the plot** to his satisfaction. It is known that he believed the book would be important for him as a writer, a way to prove that he was capable of writing more than just short stories (which he himself considered "trashy") and one popular novel. His conviction of the significance of the work made him discard the original version – published by Cambridge University Press in 2000 under its title *Trimalchio* – and work through aspects of the plot in different forms in the short stories later collected in *All the Sad Young Men*.

He continued to explore the themes which had always interested him

The themes in the novel were those which had always interested Fitzgerald as a writer and which continued to do so in his later career. The issues which inspired the "Lost Generation" – **the emptiness and search for orientation and meaning** in the wake of the First World War – are present, as are the themes of doomed love and wealth and status. The character of Gatsby, who embodies the ideal vertical progression of the American Dream from poor boy to millionaire was the perfect figure in whom to gather all these themes together and through whom Fitzgerald could write about personal subjects (love, obsession, ambition) as well as larger social issues (crime, wealth, inequality) and also tackle more abstract matters (the old and the new, changing attitudes to morality, and the American Dream itself).

Publication and title

Doubts about the title

Once he was satisfied with the arrangement of the plot, Fitzgerald reworked the book while he was in Italy in 1924. An interesting aspect of the book's writing and origins is **the trouble he had with the title**. This went through several changes, and he was apparently always unhappy with the title the book was eventually published under, calling it "rather bad than good". His preferred alternative titles were *Trimalchio* and *Under the Red, White and Blue*.

Trimalchio is the name of a character from the satirical novel *Satyricon*, by Petronius (ca. 27–66 AD). Although relatively minor – he appears in only one section of the 140 chapters in the book – **Trimalchio became a famous literary character**. He is a former slave who has been released and has become a citizen. Through hard work and determination he has acquired great wealth, which he displays in excessive feasts with many freed slaves as his guests.

The relevance to Gatsby and his parties – and the dizzy, hedonistic crowds they attract – are obvious. Fitzgerald was persuaded not to use this as a title, however, as his editor felt that the general public would not understand the reference. There is one mention of Trimalchio in the book, at the beginning of Chapter VII (p. 151 ll. 1–5), describing Gatsby's summer parties as his "career as Trimalchio". Fitzgerald's interest in this literary figure as a point of reference for his novel is interesting:

→ The use of a fictional character as a key to the central (fictional) character in a novel narrated by another fictional character (Nick Carraway) would highlight the very literary construction of the novel and suggest to readers that the character of Jay Gatsby should be understood to represent something more than just a poor boy who got rich.

→ In *The Great Gatsby* there are numerous references to Classical and ancient mythology and literature, from Plato's famous shadows on the cave wall[13] (p. 133 ll. 8–10) to the legends of the Holy Grail[14] (p. 194 ll. 15–16). These serve not only as an efficient and subtle way of connecting the story to large and complex ideas, but also help provide the surface events with a haunting depth and resonance which allows the reader to see in the characters and their actions a deeper and more universal meaning.

One other title Fitzgerald had considered was *Under the Red, White and Blue*. The significance of this is also very clear: this is a novel about American lives, American problems, American dreams. The progression of James Gatz, poor boy, to Jay Gatsby, playboy millionaire, is **the American Dream in action** – self-determination and hard work bringing success and status. But it is also shadowed by American problems: prohibition created the market for illegal alcohol and Gatsby made his money as a bootlegger, working with his Jewish-American business associate Meyer Wolfshiem. Status and wealth are material goals, but when they are achieved through crime and force, they are tainted.

Once his American dream has been realised, Gatsby is surrounded by the realities of America in the 1920s: **the shallowness and hedonism of the Jazz Age** and the jealousies and resentment between those who have wealth and those who don't, and those

---

13 In *The Republic*, the Greek philosopher Plato (424 BC–347 BC) used the allegory of people chained to a cave wall who mistake their shadows and echoes for reality to express the limits of an uneducated mind and the benefits of education and philosophy in understanding the nature of reality.

14 The Holy Grail is a mythical vessel which is linked through the legends of King Arthur to both Christian beliefs and pagan Celtic fertility rituals. In the Arthurian myths, the quest for the Grail is the greatest mission a knight can undertake.

who have "old money" (Tom Buchanan inherited his wealth) and those with "new money". There are divisions in class among those who have money – the social status of "old money" is defined by more than wealth alone. The rapid development of the pressures of modern life during the 1920s inspired a re-examination of values and identities in American literature, and this was another major theme that interested Fitzgerald.

The title Fitzgerald finally took for his novel, and with which he was never entirely happy, manages to take a step back from focusing on any one aspect of the book. While the choice of *Trimalchio* would have drawn attention to Gatsby's excessive wealth and "new money" pretensions, and *Under the Red, White and Blue* would have concentrated on the American nature of the themes, *The Great Gatsby* succeeds in broadening the scope of the reader's expectations by, paradoxically**, concentrating on the central character**. By not associating the book from the very beginning with any one particular aspect, it becomes much more accessible to interpretation. Gatsby is the focus for all the book's themes: he is the focus of the narrator's attention, the point on which the themes and conflicts of the book converge: not only a Trimalchio or an American symbol, but open to interpretation from all sides.

3.2 Summaries

In the summer of 1922, Nick Carraway takes a job in New York and rents a house on Long Island next to the mansion of a mysterious millionaire called Gatsby, who throws extravagant parties all through the summer. Nick's cousin Daisy and her wealthy husband Tom Buchanan also live on Long Island. As Nick and Gatsby get to know each other, Nick learns that Gatsby is in love with Daisy, and has been for years. They meet at Nick's house and begin an affair.
Tom is also having an affair, with Myrtle, the abused wife of poor car mechanic George Wilson, who lives in squalor in the "valley of ashes" between the fashionable resorts of Long Island and the city. One night, after Gatsby, Daisy, Tom, Nick and Nick's girlfriend Jordan have been to New York, Tom and Gatsby confront one another over Daisy's affections. Daisy, driving Gatsby's car home, kills Myrtle, who has run into the road towards the car she believes to be Tom's.
After the accident Nick learns about Gatsby's past, about his love for Daisy and how he reinvented himself and earned his wealth, all in order to win her back.
George Wilson is heartbroken and is led by Tom to believe that Gatsby was driving the car which killed Myrtle. George goes to Gatsby's house and shoots him, before turning the gun on himself.
Nick, dismayed by events and disappointed by the people he has met, organises Gatsby's funeral and then leaves the East Coast for good.

Chapter I (pp. 5–34)

The narrator Nick Carraway moves to live on Long Island near New York. His cousin Daisy and her husband Tom live nearby, and are apparently unhappy in their marriage. His neighbour is a mysterious millionaire called Gatsby.

In the first chapter we are introduced to the narrator, Nick Carraway, who presents himself as a man in whom others like to confide, as he is a tolerant and non-judgemental person. He then explains what reaction the events he is about to describe in the book had on him, and that his tolerance was tested by these events of the summer of 1922. One exception is Gatsby, for whom he feels love and sympathy, and whose romantic nature and capacity for hope he admires.

Nick briefly describes who he is and where he came from. He was born into a prominent and successful family in the Midwest[15]. He served in the First World War and came back feeling "restless" (p. 8 l. 12), leading him to leave his home and begin a career in finance. This was in the spring of 1922. Because he didn't want to live in the city itself, he ended up renting a small house in a "commuting town", West Egg on Long Island. By the summer of 1922 he is feeling like "an original settler" (p. 9 l. 23) and is enthusiastic and optimistic about the future.

His little house is next door to a huge mansion, apparently modelled on a French grand hotel, which belongs to someone called Gatsby. This mansion looks out over the water to the villas and "white palaces" (p. 12 l. 19) of East Egg, the more fashionable place to live. This is where Nick's second cousin once removed

---

15 Geographically, the states Illinois, Indiana, Iowa, Kansas, Michigan, Minnesota, Missouri, Nebraska, North Dakota, Ohio, South Dakota and Wisconsin. The Midwest has a special significance in American tradition as the 'heartland', the home of American values and traditions.

(they share a great-great-grandparent) Daisy lives with her husband Tom Buchanan, whom Nick had known in college. Tom is physically striking, a large and powerful man, who comes from an "enormously wealthy" (p. 13 ll. 8–9) family in Chicago. He and Daisy had lived in France for a year and after that had been drifting, living wherever "people were rich together" (p. 13 l. 19), and for unexplained reasons had now come to settle on the East Coast.

Daisy and Tom

Nick drives over to visit the Buchanans one evening. They live in a mansion with a huge garden. Tom greets Nick, who is struck by his "arrogant eyes" (p. 14 l. 20) and the overall impression of a "cruel body" (p. 15 l. 8). Tom is clearly an arrogant, restless man with whom Nick has a strangely unaffectionate friendship.

Tom shows Nick around his mansion and they find Daisy and a friend of hers whom Nick doesn't know, later introduced as Jordan Baker. Daisy is a charming and delicate woman, "sad and lovely" (p. 18 l. 17), a woman who obviously knows the effect she has on men and enjoys exploiting it by adopting an innocent and helpless manner. She is playfully self-centred and combines a kind of childishness with the sophistication of the elite. She questions Nick about where he has been and what he has been doing and mentions that she has a child. Tom interrupts the conversation to ask Nick about what work he's doing: during this interruption he makes it clear that he and Daisy will be staying in the East. He glances at Daisy when he says that he would be a fool to live anywhere else.

Gatsby is mentioned

Jordan at this point joins in and Nick is interested in her, and thinks he has seen her face somewhere. She knows that he lives in West Egg and asks if he knows Gatsby: Daisy reacts to the name. There is no time to learn more as dinner is announced.

During the course of the evening Nick observes that Daisy and Tom are not happy with one another. Nick is interested in Daisy and Jordan's cool sophistication, which is so different from conversation in the world in which he grew up. He tells Daisy that she makes him feel "uncivilized" (p. 23 l. 6), setting Tom on a rant about the decay of civilization and the decline of the white race. His racist lecture – he does not react to obvious signs from the others that they are not interested in or don't agree with his ideas – is interrupted by a telephone call. When Tom leaves the room to take the call Daisy becomes almost desperately close and attentive. There is a distinct feeling in the room of being momentarily freed of Tom's brutish, unpleasant and commanding presence. Daisy abruptly leaves: when they are left alone, Jordan tells Nick that Tom is having an affair with "some woman in New York" (p. 26 ll. 14–15).

Daisy and Tom return but then the telephone rings again: Daisy signals to Tom that he shouldn't answer it. Later on, after dinner, Daisy and Nick are talking and she confides to him that she has become cynical, and that the way she sees the world now is that the best thing a girl can be in this world is a "beautiful little fool" (p. 29 l. 8). Nick is unsettled by her manipulative sophistication and the disturbing undercurrent of emotions between her and Tom.

The night carries on: Nick realises that Jordan Baker, who is now leaving, is indeed familiar: she is a professional golfer who was associated with some unpleasantness now long forgotten. Daisy makes a fuss about setting the two of them up as a couple. After she leaves Daisy and Tom continue their sarcastic bickering. Nick sets off and as he is leaving Daisy asks if it is true that he is engaged: it isn't, and he leaves.

The green light

On the way home Nick feels "confused and a little disgusted" (p. 33 ll. 2–3). The evening has upset him, and when he is back at his house that night he sits in the garden and looks out over the water. He sees a figure at the mansion next door, whom he assumes to be his neighbour, Gatsby, and watches him reach out his arms towards a green light on the other side of the water before vanishing.

Cover of the first edition, 1925. © ullstein bild – The Granger Collection

Chapter II (pp. 34–56)

Tom and Nick go to New York: on the way they pick up Tom's mistress, Myrtle Wilson. They throw a drunken, confused party that afternoon in the city. Tom breaks Myrtle's nose during an argument about Daisy.

The valley of ashes and the giant eyes

Nick describes the "valley of ashes" (repeatedly used to describe the location, but first appearing on p. 34 l. 25), a place halfway between West Egg and New York where the railroad line and the road converge along a desolate stretch of land which is used as a dumping ground for ash. This hopeless, ugly and lifeless place is watched over by a huge billboard advertising the optician Doctor T.J. Eckleburg. The giant blue eyes on the billboard look from behind a pair of glasses but there is no face. The original cover of the novel echoed this image, which acquires great significance as the novel progresses, replacing the optician's disembodied eyes with a woman's eyes.

Tom and Nick are going to New York one afternoon on the train, and when they reach the valley of ashes, where the train must pause to allow barges to pass on the river, Tom insists that Nick should meet his mistress. His demand is aggressive and Nick follows him under the eyes of the billboard to a small building in which George Wilson has a small garage where he buys, sells and repairs cars.

George and Myrtle

There they meet George and Myrtle Wilson. George wants to buy Tom's car – this is obviously a long-standing wish – but Tom treats him cruelly. Myrtle is fixated on Tom and treats George as if he were invisible. When he leaves the room briefly Myrtle and Tom make a date to meet that afternoon. Outside the garage, Tom tells Nick that it does Myrtle good to get away from this "terrible place" (p. 39 l. 22), and that George doesn't object because he doesn't know – "He's so dumb he doesn't know he's alive." (p. 40 l. 3)

Nick, Tom and Myrtle take the train to New York. Tom spoils her, buying her anything she wants, including a small dog. Nick tries to get away from them but Tom insists that he join them in their apartment. When they get to the apartment Tom gets a bottle of whiskey and Myrtle calls a lot of people on the telephone: soon there is a party in full swing. Myrtle's sister Catherine is there, as are some neighbours from the house, the McKees. Myrtle changes costume and her personality seems to change as well during the party: she becomes "more violently affected" (p. 46 l. 12) and influences the atmosphere in the apartment.

Myrtle's party

The party is a drunken, claustrophobic, hysterical affair, and the people are crude and badly behaved. Gatsby is mentioned: there is a rumour that he is related in some way to Kaiser Wilhelm. Catherine tells Nick that it is Daisy's fault that Tom and Myrtle can't leave their respective spouses and marry. Nick tries to leave but is forced to stay. Myrtle seizes him and tells him how she first met Tom. The heart of it – a chance meeting on a train – seems to be her submission to the sheer force of Tom's will and physical presence.

The party goes on and on and Nick's sense of time becomes unreliable. At some point Tom and Myrtle are arguing about Daisy and he slaps her in the face, breaking her nose. In the confusion Nick seizes his chance and follows Mr. McKee when he leaves the apartment. Events become more disorientated. The chapter ends with Nick waking up in the railway station, cold and alone, waiting for the 4.30 train back to Long Island.

Chapter III (pp. 56–84)

Gatsby hosts large parties at his house all through the summer. Nick is invited to one where he meets Jordan Baker again, and is involved in a conversation with a man who turns out to be Jay Gatsby. At the end of the night there is a car crash outside Gatsby's house.

Gatsby's parties

Because he lives next door, Nick can observe the preparations for Gatsby's parties and the parties themselves: there is music and dancing all night long, guests gathering in the afternoon, ferried across the water in Gatsby's own motor boats, brought from the city in his Rolls Royce and brought to the house from the railway station in his yellow station wagon. Before the parties – at least once every fortnight – streams of caterers bring the food and drink and set up marquees, buffets and bars. The music is provided by an entire orchestra. After the weekends eight extra servants are needed to clear up the mess of the parties. Nick has been able to watch the parties as they develop, the crowds of people who revel in the music, dancing, drinking and atmosphere of freedom and fun in the huge house and its gardens.

He is invited one Saturday. He soon realises that he is one of the few people who was actually invited. He feels initially uncomfortable among crowds of people he doesn't know, before running into Jordan Baker. They wander together before settling at a table with some other guests who are talking about Gatsby – stories about his extravagant generosity and darker rumours about his past. Some say he killed a man, or that he was a German spy during the war.

Gatsby appears

Jordan and Nick search for Gatsby. They find a drunken, owl-eyed man in the library who is astonished that the books are real. They go back outside where the dancing has started: by now Nick is enjoying himself. A man who is sharing their table says Nick looks familiar, and asks him if he served in a particular division during the war: it turns out that this man is Jay Gatsby. He is roughly the same age as Nick – around thirty – and he makes a very positive first impression. Just as Gatsby has introduced himself, a butler appears to tell him that Chicago is calling him on the telephone. When he is gone he asks Jordan who he is and what he does: she says that Gatsby told her he once that he was an "Oxford man", but that she doesn't believe it.

The party continues with more dancing and entertainment. The butler reappears and asks Jordan to come and see Gatsby. Left alone again Nick wanders around the party which is becoming more drunken, with fights and squabbles breaking out among couples. Nick is just getting ready to leave when Jordan and Gatsby reappear from the library. She tells Nick that she has just heard something amazing: she asks him to come and visit her at her aunt's, and then she leaves. Nick is saying goodbye to Gatsby, who has invited him to come out the next day to take a ride in his hydroplane when the butler interrupts again with another telephone call, this time from Philadelphia. On his way out of the house Nick sees that there has been a car accident involving the owl-eyed man from the library.

The chapter then shifts to Nick's life. He points out that the events he has been describing are not the only things which were occupying him during those weeks. He talks about his work, briefly mentions having had an affair with a girl from the accounting department, and describes his routines. He now likes New York, and describes his impressions of the city and the changes it goes through during the day.

He and Jordan are spending time together, and while he doesn't love her, he is interested and fond of her. He realises that she is a deeply dishonest person who cannot stand losing or being at a disadvantage. Nick wants to officially finish the relationship he has with a girl from back home before he can move on with Jordan: he comments that his virtue is honesty.

Chapter IV (pp. 84–111)

Nick visits Gatsby's house and Gatsby tells him about what he did during the war. In the city they meet Gatsby's friend Mayer Wolfshiem. Later, Jordan tells Nick about Daisy's affair with Gatsby and her marriage to Tom.

Nick makes a long list of people he has seen at Gatsby's parties, and he hears more rumours about the mysterious Gatsby – that he is a bootlegger, that he killed someone, that he is related to the German military leader (and later President) von Hindenburg.

Late in July Gatsby turns up at Nick's house in his "gorgeous car" (p. 88 l. 10) and takes him to lunch in New York. During the drive Gatsby demands to known what Nick thinks of him: he says that he wants to correct the impression Nick may have got from the wild stories which are circulating. Claiming to tell "God's truth" (p. 90 l. 12), Gatsby goes on to tell Nick his story. The son of wealthy people from the Midwest, he was raised in the US but educated at Oxford University in England, which he say is a family tradition. Nick is suspicious: he agrees with Jordan's assessment that Gatsby is lying when he says he studied at Oxford. He is also suspiciously vague about where he came from – the Midwest or San Francisco? He claims to have lived for a while in various European capitals and describes a lifestyle that Nick finds too clichéd to believe. Gatsby also mentions a very sad event in his past which he has been trying to forget.

Then, says Gatsby, he went to war: he talks about his time serving in the army and the promotions and medals he won. He has a medal with him in the car which he shows to Nick, awarded to him by the government of Montenegro. He also has a photograph of himself at what appears to be one of the Oxford colleges. Nick is finally convinced that Gatsby has been telling the truth about his extraordinary past and fabulous career.

Gatsby wants to ask Nick for a favour. He says that he usually feels alone among strangers because he drifts around so much in an effort to "forget the sad thing" (p. 94 l. 6) that happened to him. Gatsby has arranged to have Jordan Baker tell Nick about this mysterious matter later that day, which annoys Nick, as he feels that Gatsby is involving himself in his relationship with Jordan. On their way into the city they pass through the valley of ashes and Nick sees George Wilson working at his garage.

They meet Gatsby's friend and business partner Mayer Wolfshiem in a restaurant in the city, where he at first mistakes Nick for another potential partner. He speaks openly about his connections to the criminal underworld. Gatsby later tells Nick that he is a gambler who was responsible for manipulating the 1919 baseball World Series. Gatsby rushes off to make a telephone call, and in his absence Wolfshiem tells Nick how much he likes Gatsby and, seemingly unconnected to anything that has been said, makes a point of Gatsby's careful behaviour around women. When Gatsby returns Wolfshiem leaves, and Nick spots Tom Buchanan in the restaurant as well. When Nick introduces them Gatsby seems embarrassed. He then vanishes.

The story of Daisy and Gatsby

In the afternoon Nick meets Jordan who tells him how, in 1917, Daisy and Gatsby first met. He was following her around, as were many young men. She only saw them together briefly, but she remembered the incident because of the romantic intensity with which Gatsby was watching Daisy. There was a rumour that Daisy's mother had found her trying to run away to say goodbye to a soldier who was leaving the country. After a quiet period she became her usual lively self again and married Tom in a flashy and expensive ceremony (he apparently gave her jewellery worth $350.000).

Jordan was a bridesmaid at the wedding and tells Nick how on the day before the wedding she found Daisy holding a letter, drunk and desperate, saying she had changed her mind. Jordan managed to tidy her up and she went through with the marriage. She seemed to be in love with Tom until one August when Tom was involved in a car accident, and a young woman who was with him in the car was injured. The Buchanans moved around a lot in France before returning to Chicago. And then a few weeks ago Jordan had mentioned Gatsby and Daisy had remembered him.

Jordan then tells Nick that Gatsby had bought the huge mansion just so he could be near Daisy. She asks him for the favour Gatsby had requested: he would like Nick to invite Daisy to his house and then let Gatsby come over. Nick is surprised at how simple the request is, compared to the massive efforts Gatsby has made in buying the mansion and throwing the fabulous parties just to get Daisy‘s attention. One condition for this meeting is that Daisy must not know that Gatsby will be there.

Chapter V (pp. 111–131)

Nick arranges the meeting between Daisy and Gatsby at his house. They then all go to Gatsby's mansion where he shows Daisy his possessions, including his wardrobes full of expensive imported clothes.

Nick returns home and sees that all the lights are on in Gatsby‘s house. Gatsby is impatient to hear if Nick has spoken to Jordan about his request. They agree to have the meeting on the day after next. Gatsby then offers Nick some work, a "confidential sort of thing" (p. 113 ll. 27–28) which Nick politely declines. The next day, Nick invites Daisy over, warning her not to bring Tom.

Daisy and Gatsby reunited

On the day itself there is rain, and Gatsby sends over his gardener to cut the grass at Nick's house. He then turns up himself, nervous, pale and anxious. Just as he is about to leave, disappointed, Daisy arrives. Gatsby hides while Nick welcomes Daisy, and reappears at the front door, "pale as death" (p. 117 l. 20), and heads straight for the living room where Daisy is waiting. Nick is made very uncomfortable by the intense atmosphere between the two of them, the "clear artificial note" (p. 118 ll. 6–7) in Daisy's voice and Gatsby's "counterfeit of perfect ease" (p. 118 ll. 12–13). When Nick says he is going to leave them alone Gatsby panics and says that he has made "a terrible mistake" (p. 120 l. 1), at which Nick loses patience and tells him he is acting like a child. He leaves them alone and stands under the shelter of a tree in the rain for half an hour.

When he returns he sees that Daisy has been crying and Gatsby is literally glowing: "a new well-being radiated from him" (p. 122 ll. 4–6). Gatsby wants to show Daisy his house and asks Nick to come along as well. Gatsby guides them around the house and Nick sees that the only value the house and possessions have for him depends on Daisy's responses. He has gone from being embarrassed to being wildly happy to now being stunned by her presence. He begins showing her his clothes, explaining that he has "a man in England" (p. 126 l. 10) who buys his clothes for him. Daisy is overwhelmed – by the beauty of the shirts, she says.

They take a tour of the grounds and the swimming pool. Gatsby mentions that, when it isn't raining, he can see a green light on her dock. Nick finds a photograph of an old man; this is Dan Cody, Gatsby tells him: "he used to be my best friend" (p. 127 l. 28). Daisy and Gatsby are wrapped up in each other and have forgotten Nick. He leaves them alone and goes back to his house.

Chapter VI (pp. 131–150)

Gatsby's notoriety is spreading and Nick explains his true history, as told to him by Gatsby. Tom and Daisy attend one of Gatsby's parties: afterwards Gatsby is worried that she didn't like it. Nick understands that Gatsby is obsessed with Daisy and with his own past.

A reporter comes to Nick's house asking about Gatsby. It turns out that the rumours which have been flying around have awakened some real interest, and that his romantic appeal is becoming a kind of notoriety as he is linked to illegal alcohol smuggling from Canada into the US ("the underground pipe-line to Canada", p. 132 ll. 10–11). Nick then tells the story of Gatsby's past, as told by Gatsby. Gatsby was born James Gatz, the poor son of a poor family from North Dakota. He had his name legally changed to Jay Gatsby when he was 17. He had met a multi-millionaire called Dan Cody, who was charmed by the quick-witted and ambitious young man and employed him for five years. Gatsby was supposed to have inherited $25.000 from Cody when the old man died, but a greedy woman called Ella Kaye had outmanoeuvred him and taken all the money.

Tom and Daisy come to Gatsby's party

After telling this story Nick says that he has not seen Gatsby for weeks, as he has been spending time with Jordan. He goes to visit Gatsby one Sunday when Tom Buchanan turns up with two other people. The situation is awkward and Tom obviously doesn't approve of Gatsby. The next weekend, however, Tom and Daisy come to Gatsby's party, and his presence, Nick thinks, makes this particular evening different from the others – it has a "peculiar quality of oppressiveness" (p. 141 l. 8). The same people as always are there but Nick feels "an unpleasantness in the air, a pervading harshness" (p. 141 ll. 13–14). Daisy is obviously not enjoying herself unless she is with Gatsby, who is called away to answer a telephone call. They sit at a table with drunken guests and Daisy is offended by their crude and pointless conversations. While he and Daisy are waiting to leave, Tom asks if Gatsby is a bootlegger (an alcohol smuggler): he assumes that many of the "newly rich" are bootleggers. Daisy tells him that he actually set up a chain of drug stores.

Gatsby's obsession with the past

Gatsby has asked Nick to stay on after the party. He is worried that Daisy didn't enjoy herself. Nick warns him not to try to repeat the past, but this is exactly what Gatsby wants to do, Nick realises: to reinvent the past, with himself as a rich boy so that Daisy will be able to love him. His love for Daisy, as seen in the "appalling sentimentality" (p. 150 ll. 16–17) of his memories, is unreal, expressed in terms of transcendence and mysticism.

Chapter VII (pp. 151–191)

After a lunch at Tom and Daisy's house with Gatsby, Jordan and Nick, they all drive into New York and rent a suite at the Plaza Hotel. There is an argument between Tom and Gatsby over Daisy and Tom accuses Gatsby of being a criminal. He sends Gatsby and Daisy back home, knowing he has won. On their way home Tom, Nick and Jordan see that Myrtle Wilson has been run over and killed. Nick learns that Daisy had been driving the car and is responsible for Myrtle's death.

The parties at Gatsby's house come to an end. Nick goes over to see if Gatsby is alright and meets his new, unfriendly staff. The next day Gatsby calls him and tells Nick that because Daisy comes over to his house regularly he wanted new servants (provided by Wolfshiem) who wouldn't gossip. Nick believes that, because Daisy signalled some kind of disapproval, Gatsby has simply thrown away everything – the parties, the lifestyle, and his serving staff.

The real reason for calling Nick though is to invite him to lunch at Daisy's.

As Nick arrives Tom is on the telephone: Jordan, who has also been invited, tells him that it is "Tom's girl" – Myrtle. When Nick overhears what Tom is saying, though, it becomes clear that it's George he is talking to. Tom greets Gatsby, but as soon as he leaves the room gain Daisy rushes over and kisses Gatsby and tells him she loves him. Her daughter is then brought in and displayed.

After lunch Daisy suggests that they all go to New York: she compliments Gatsby so blatantly that Tom realises she is in love with him. Having decided to go to New York, they arrange that Tom – who makes pointed comments about drug stores, obviously having learned something sinister about Gatsby's money – will take Nick and Jordan in Gatsby's car. Daisy and Gatsby take Tom's car. Tom stops for fuel at Wilson's garage. George is obviously ill and depressed. He is in desperate need of money, he says, and asks again if he can buy Tom's car. He wants to get enough money so he and Myrtle can move out West. George says he has become suspicious about "something funny" (p. 164 l. 24) going on – presumably Myrtle being involved with another man. Tom and George both know that their wives are having affairs. Nick sees Myrtle staring from her window at the car and he knows she is staring at Jordan, whom she obviously assumes to be Tom's wife.

Myrtle sees Tom in Gatsby's car

In the city they decide, after an argument, to rent a suite at the Plaza Hotel. Tom begins to challenge Gatsby when Gatsby tells him to stop bothering Daisy. She tries to divert them from arguing but this only works for a few minutes. Tom has decided to attack Gatsby's claim to have been at Oxford: it turns out some American officers were able to attend English and French universities after the war. Tom is not pleased that Gatsby has an explanation and attacks him more directly. Gatsby responds equally directly: "Your

The confrontation between Tom and Gatsby

wife doesn't love you … She loves me." (p. 173 ll. 10–11). Tom is unimpressed, he says he doesn't care about the history of five years ago, and that he and Daisy love each other. Daisy is forced to respond, and Nick sees that she never really wanted it to go so far. Gatsby wants her to tell Tom that she never loved him, that she had always loved Gatsby, but she can't – "Oh, you want too much!" (p. 175 l. 26). She had loved Tom, and he says that the two of them have shared things Gatsby can never know.

Tom has investigated Gatsby and knows that he is involved with Meyer Wolfshiem in selling illegal alcohol through the drug stores they bought, and also implies that Gatsby is involved with illegal gambling. Tom has won. Gatsby tries to defend himself but Daisy is withdrawing, too scared to act. Tom tells the two of them to drive back home in Gatsby's car. He is contemptuous of Gatsby's "presumptuous little flirtation" (p. 179 l. 2). Nick realises that today is his birthday; he has just turned thirty.

Myrtle's death

Tom drives Nick and Jordan back to Long Island. On the way they pass a crowd gathered around Wilson's garage, where they learn that Myrtle has been killed by a car. They find out from onlookers that it had been a fast, yellow car – Gatsby's. Tom makes sure that George Wilson, who is deeply upset, understands that the yellow car he had seen Tom in earlier was not his, and that he is not responsible for Myrtle's death.

Nick just wants to get away from all of them, including Jordan, and is waiting for a taxi outside the Buchanans' house when he sees Gatsby hiding in the darkness. Nick soon finds out that Daisy had been driving; she has killed Myrtle Wilson. He wants to stay outside their house tonight to make sure Tom doesn't hurt Daisy. Nick sneaks up to the house to see what is going on and watches Tom and Daisy sitting together, apparently conspiring. He leaves Gatsby outside the house, "watching over nothing". (p. 191 l. 7).

Chapter VIII (pp. 191–210)

Gatsby tells Nick the story of how he and Daisy fell in love. Afterwards Nick leaves, saying goodbye to Gatsby. George Wilson is in shock after Myrtle's death: he goes to Gatsby's house, where he shoots him and then kills himself.

Gatsby's story

On the morning after Myrtle's death, Nick goes over to Gatsby's house, which seems empty and ghostly. Gatsby tells him about Dan Cody (the story which is told by Nick on pp. 132–7) and talks about Daisy. He tells Nick how he fell in love with her, what it was about her that fascinated him. She became a "grail" (p. 194 l. 16), a mythical and unreachable symbol of purity and salvation. And then, after a month together, he was sent away to the war, where he did very well and was awarded several medals and quickly promoted. Daisy was left in her "artificial world" (p. 196 l. 12) and gradually became distant. She was courted and swept away by Tom Buchanan and with "a certain struggle and a certain relief" (p. 197 ll. 11–12) she split from Gatsby and married Tom.

It is now autumn and the gardener wants to drain the swimming pool: Gatsby tells him not to, he hasn't used it himself at all and he wants to swim at least once. Nick has to leave, but he feels that he shouldn't leave Gatsby alone: he tells Gatsby that he is worth more than all the "rotten crowd" (p. 200 l. 14) – meaning Tom, Daisy, Jordan, Wolfshiem, and all the party guests – and says goodbye. Nick goes to work but is tired and falls asleep. Jordan calls him in his office and they argue. He then tries to call Gatsby but no one answers. He then explains what had happened the night before, after he, Jordan and Tom had left Wilson's garage.

George after Myrtle's death

Michaelis, the young man who runs the coffee shop near George Wilson's garage, stayed with George through the night. At around 3 a.m. George began talking about the yellow car – Gatsby's, which

Daisy had been driving – saying that he knew how to find out who had been driving. He has found out that Myrtle is involved with someone and Michaelis sees that he is nearly mad with grief and anger. He begins talking about the eyes of God (p. 207) but he is staring at the billboard with Doctor Eckleburg's eyes.

Later that morning – at around 10 a.m. – Wilson has disappeared. His movements have been reconstructed, probably by the police, and Nick explains how he walked to a place called Gad's Hill, with witnesses being able to account for his activities until midday. Then he disappears for three hours and no one can find out where he was or what he was doing. At half past two he is seen again, now in West Egg, asking where Gatsby's house is.

George kills Gatsby and himself

Gatsby has decided to go swimming for the first time in his pool. While he is in the pool on a rubber mattress George walks out of the grounds and shoots him dead and then kills himself. Nick, who has been having premonitions about something terrible awaiting Gatsby, rushes to the house where he and some of Wolfshiem's people find Gatsby and George both dead.

Chapter IX (pp. 211–233)

After Gatsby's death Nick is left to organise the funeral. Gatsby's father, Henry Gatz, arrives. Only Nick, Henry Gatz and "Owl Eyes" attend the funeral. Disappointed by the people he has met here, Nick decides to leave and return to his home in the West.

Looking back from a distance of two years, Nick says that he has difficulty remembering all the details of the day of Gatsby's murder. He is surprised and pleased that Myrtle Wilson's sister Catherine never mentions Myrtle's affair with Tom, which allows the investigators to keep the whole case as simple as possible – George Wilson was obviously insane. Nick is the only person left on Gatsby's side. He realises that no one else is interested, and no one else cares. He tries to call Daisy but she and Tom have already disappeared. He can't reach Meyer Wolfshiem either. He feels Gatsby speaking to him, asking Nick to get somebody for him: "I can't go through this alone" (p. 213 ll. 20–21).

He receives a letter from Wolfshiem the next day which makes him angry, because the old man says he can't come because of important business. Nick then receives a strange telephone call from a man who is obviously involved with Gatsby's criminal activities.

Gatsby's father arrives

On the third day after the death Gatsby's father, Mr Henry Gatz, arrives. He is sad at the death of his son Jimmy, but also extremely proud of what he achieved – the huge house and the vast wealth. He is convinced that, had he lived, his son would have become a great man who would have helped build the country. Nick, knowing that this is not true, feels uncomfortable.

On the day of the funeral Nick goes to find Meyer Wolfshiem in New York. He has difficulty getting into the office, but when he does Wolfshiem tells him about his history with Gatsby. He claims to have "made him" (p. 221 l. 4). He says he can't come to the funeral – he never gets involved when there has been a murder. He advises Nick: "Let us learn to show our friendship for a man when he is alive and not after he is dead" (p. 222 II. 10–11), and Nick leaves and returns to Gatsby's house.

The schedule for self-improvement

Henry Gatz shows him a book where the young Gatsby had written down a schedule self-improvement, precisely listing activities he wanted to do every day in order to better himself both physically and mentally.

The funeral

The only people attending the funeral are Nick, Henry Gatz, a few servants, the postman from West Egg, and the owl-eyed man Nick had met in Gatsby's library earlier in the summer. Nick recalls his vivid memories of returning to the West by train from school:

"this has been a story of the West, after all – Tom and Gatsby, Daisy and Jordan and I, were all Westerners, and perhaps we possessed some deficiency in common which made us subtly unadaptable to Eastern life" (p. 227 ll. 12–16). He decides to return home to the West, and describes a dream-vision of the East: four men in flashy clothes carry a drunken woman in evening dress into the wrong house, and no one knows or cares who she is. Before he leaves he wants to end things cleanly with Jordan. She is engaged to marry someone else now. He feels half in love with her but leaves.

Last meeting with Tom

Later that autumn, in October, Nick meets Tom by accident on the street. He is quite blunt about how much he dislikes him and, acting on a hunch, asks Tom what he said to Wilson on the day of the murder. His guess is correct: Wilson had gone to see Tom, who had told him about Gatsby. This is what happened during those hours of the day of the murder the police had not been able to reconstruct. Nick knows that the tragedy is that it wasn't Gatsby who had been driving and killed Myrtle, but there is nothing he can say now. Nick realises that Tom and Daisy are "careless people ... they smashed up things and creatures and then retreated back into their money" (p. 231 ll. 15–17).

Before leaving the East, Nick returns to Gatsby's house. He thinks about what has happened and about how Gatsby's dream was doomed, and about how we all, in chasing dreams which are born in the past, are unable to move onwards into the future.

3.3 Structure

The novel is unusual in that it doesn't, strictly speaking, have a single centre: Nick Carraway, Jay Gatsby, or Daisy Buchanan? The storyteller, the tragic central figure, or the focus of the characters' obsessions?

Person at the centre

The centre of the novel

Because Nick is both a character and an observer, and because the entire story is arranged and told by him, he cannot be pushed to the sidelines. But *The Great Gatsby* is not really Nick's story. Despite the events which concern him directly – the relationship with Jordan, for example – **he is intimately involved in someone else's tragedy**. And although the book bears his name, and his story and character is at the heart of the novel, Gatsby is himself just one corner in the love triangle which makes the novel's plot, and his own story is a mystery which forms the background to the events of the summer.

Considering the network of relationships and the focus of the various obsessions and events in the novel, the most efficient map to include all the characters has Daisy Buchanan, the tragically hollow object and focus of the novel's events, at its centre:

Daisy at the centre

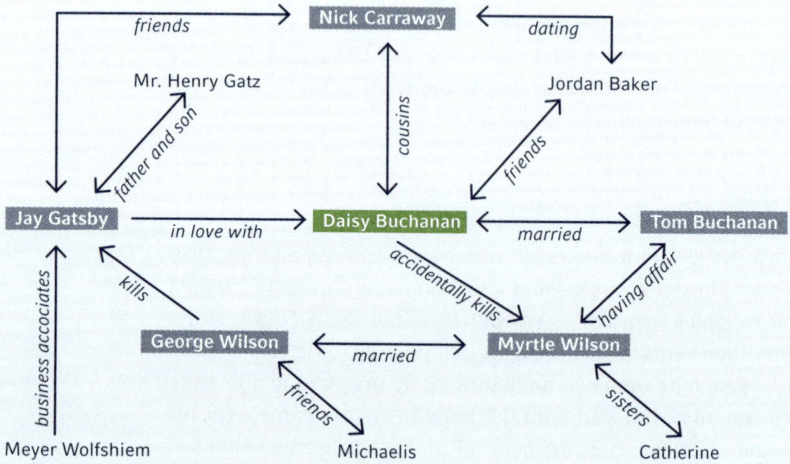

→ Nick as narrator and Mr Henry Gatz as grieving parent transcend the murky mess of events.

→ On the right hand side then are the clear-cut, hard figures: the cynical, sophisticated Jordan, the arrogant, thuggish Tom, and the shallow and crude Myrtle.

→ Daisy is the apex of the love triangle: her desirability inspires Gatsby's unreal dreams, and as his wife she is within Tom's possessive sphere.

→ Nick is the narrator and as such must be positioned above the others in a position from which, as in the text, he can access their various viewpoints in telling the story.

An alternative, reduced character map clarifies the central, most relevant action of the novel, the messy tragedy of infidelity and death:

Tom at the centre

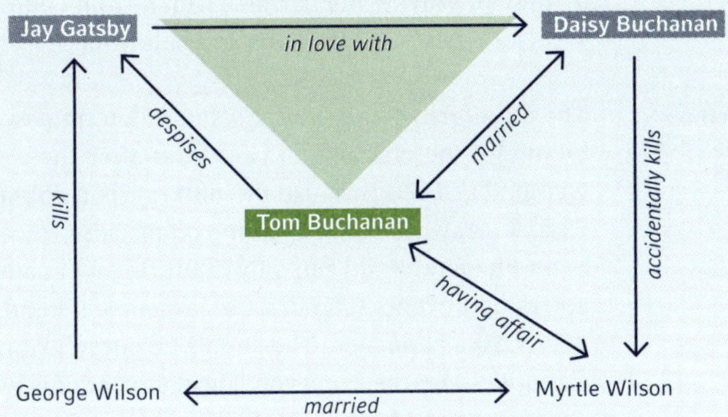

All other characters in this approach are peripheral.

→ In this character map it is Tom who is central, as it is he who brings the Wilsons into contact with Daisy – who kills Myrtle – and Gatsby – who is killed by George. When we concentrate on the plot of the summer of 1922, all the other characters are truly secondary to this central web of deceit and death. The love triangle of the wealthy and self-obsessed characters Daisy, Tom and Gatsby is situated above the poverty and despair of the doomed Wilsons. The infidelities – Tom and Myrtle and Daisy and Gatsby – create the web holding these characters together.

→ Nick and Jordan are tools used to reunite Gatsby and Daisy – something which, given Gatsby's will power and obsession, would have happened anyway: Jordan tells Nick (p. 109 ll. 9–13) that it was no coincidence that Gatsby bought a house so near to where Daisy lived.
→ All other characters in this approach are peripheral, serving only to provide the narrator with insights into the central characters' pasts, motivations and behaviour.

The narrator's role in structuring the novel

The structure of *The Great Gatsby* is determined by how it is told: by one of the characters, two years after the events it describes (see p. 211 l. 2). Because the narrator is a character in the novel (Nick Carraway) rather than the omniscient voice of the author (F. Scott Fitzgerald), he can only interpret and comment on the characters and events – he can't read people's minds or explain why things have happened. The people he doesn't know – Dan Cody, for example – and the events he doesn't experience – George Wilson's anguish after Myrtle's death, Gatsby's first meeting with Daisy, George's murder of Gatsby – have to be reconstructed from things he learns at a later date from other characters. Because the narrator, Nick, is telling this story two years later, and because his story includes not only his own observations and experiences but those of other people (most importantly Gatsby, Jordan and Michaelis), Fitzgerald can arrange the elements and perspectives of his novel in the most satisfying and entertainingly way possible. Therefore we as readers don't know everything from the beginning. Nick suggests certain things – Gatsby's shady life, his disappointment with the immorality of what he had seen – which, positioned as they are at the very beginning of the novel, are designed to awaken the reader's interest in mysterious and possibly tragic events.

- → We know that Gatsby is somehow doomed, but not how or why.
- → We learn, only gradually and tantalisingly, about Gatsby's shady criminal career, from rumours and whispers at his parties via his own heavily edited version to, finally, the full truth.
- → We learn about the origins of the love between Daisy and Gatsby from various sources
- → We are led by Fitzgerald, through Nick's unfolding story, to an understanding of the shallow destructiveness of Daisy and Tom in their careless arrogance, although it is suggested at the beginning.

Nick does not tell the story chronologically, or entirely from his own perspective: certain key passages are reconstructed from other characters' viewpoints. Nick is not an infallible, omniscient narrator: he is himself a character in the novel with feelings, thoughts, and a life of his own, as he makes clear in Chapter III (p. 79 ll. 19–24) when he reminds the reader that he, Nick Carraway, has a life outside the events surrounding Gatsby and the Buchanans. He admits that the events immediately following Gatsby's murder are a blur about which he can remember very little (p. 211 ll. 2–5). The presence of a narrator who is more than merely a clinical observer, yet who is not himself at the centre of events, allows Fitzgerald to involve the reader in a much more complex manner. The reader is encouraged to examine and interpret the characters and events from at least two perspectives, because they are delivered through the filter of Nick's re-telling. Nick, as a writer writing within a novel, can add a layer of literary structure to the story.

Diverse voices

Another important aspect of having Nick narrate the novel in fragments of his own and others' impressions is the great variety of expression, atmosphere and tone that this allows. Instead of being restricted to the monotone of a single voice and attitude we have a choreography of perspectives, from the cooler, drier account of George Wilson's last day in Chapter VIII to the poetic sentimentalism of Gatsby's own memories (pp. 149–150), all balanced by Nick's literary and reflective prose.

Controlling the information available to the reader

The structure of Nick's narration is defined by how much or how little we the readers learn about Gatsby. The character must remain mysterious to keep our attention, but must also become human enough to make his story meaningful. Given the facts of Gatsby's life it would have been easy to present him as either a comical figure, a love-blind clown, or a much more sinister criminal figure. Similarly, if the reader is not given enough information about the man, then we are left with a mere symbol personifying certain themes – the American Dream, the lust for wealth and status, the shallowness of the pursuit of these things – whose death would be a mechanical inevitability of his symbolic function. But as Gatsby has been revealed through Nick's multi-layered narration in careful episodes, he remains mysterious and tantalising while gradually being fleshed out and becoming increasingly interesting and sympathetic as a rounded character.

Scenic construction

Another rich aspect of the structure of the novel is the scenic construction. There are certain richly detailed set pieces, carefully placed in the structure of the novel to reflect and comment on one another. Examples include:

→ Myrtle and Tom's party in Chapter II and its reflection in the gathering at the Plaza Hotel in Chapter VII
→ The larger parties in Gatsby's house in Chapters III and VI

→ The reunion of Daisy and Gatsby at Nick's house in the centre of the book (Chapter V)
→ The recollections of key events from the past coming from different sources (Jordan and Gatsby).

The echoing or reflection of events is a typical feature of *The Great Gatsby*. Opposites (Myrtle–Daisy, Gatsby–Tom, Gatsby–George) are carefully established through Nick's narration (for example his impressions of Daisy and Myrtle) as well as through the juxtaposition of scenes.

Cinematic techniques

In describing these scenes Fitzgerald has Nick Carraway use almost cinematic methods. The more intimate party at Myrtle's flat and the gathering in the Plaza are very finely observed and detailed, like a close-up camera shot in a film. The larger parties at Gatsby's mansion are much more panoramic in scale and in style: the reader's attention is guided through the day's preparations and around the extensive grounds with the dancing area and the buffet tables and the long list of guests.

Cyclical structure

The structure of the novel is fittingly cyclical. We begin with Nick looking back on the summer of 1922 and move through to the end of that summer and his return home. When we consider that one of the major themes is that of the past, and of Gatsby's efforts to recreate or re-imagine the past, this cyclical structure makes sense. While the origins are in the summer of 1917, when Daisy first met Gatsby, or maybe even earlier, when James Gatz became Jay Gatsby, Nick is concerned with how these past events created the events of 1922.

The major events described in the novel can be seen as points around a circle, beginning with Nick looking back from "now" on his arrival in Long Island "then", and returning to that point – Nick looking back on 1922 from "now".

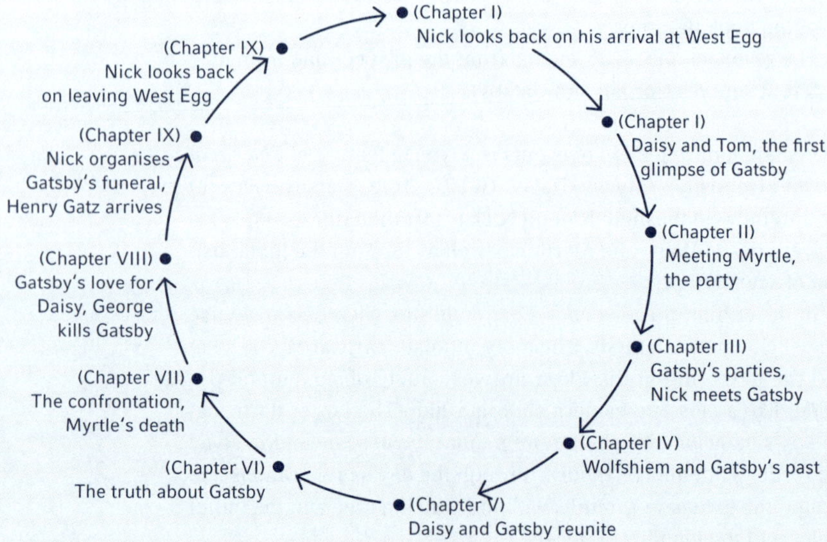

This circular structure surrounds, describes and is fed by the mystery of Gatsby's origins and his love for Daisy: the hopes and dreams that motivated him.

3.4 The Characters: Constellations and Characteristics

The central characters

Nick Carraway

- → The narrator and a friend of Gatsby
- → 30 years old, level-headed, an observer of human nature
- → Cousin to Daisy, old acquaintance of Tom, friend to Jay Gatsby, and romantically involved with Jordan Baker
- → The only person on Gatsby's side at the end

Jay Gatsby

- → Born poor as James Gatz, he reinvents himself and grows wealthy with illegal bootlegging and gambling
- → In love with Daisy and, apart from Nick, seems to have no real friends
- → Obsessed with self-improvement and with the dreams of his past
- → Killed by George in a case of mistaken identity

Daisy Buchanan

- → The beautiful, wealthy wife of Tom, she is Gatsby's great love
- → Selfish and reliant on male attention
- → Betrays Tom with Gatsby and then rejects Gatsby for Tom's wealth and power
- → Kills Myrtle Wilson in a hit-and-run car accident

Tom Buchanan

→ Wealthy upper-class heir
→ Arrogant, brutish, racist and violent, treats other people with contempt
→ Has an affair with Myrtle
→ Indirectly responsible for the deaths of Myrtle, George and Gatsby

Jordan Baker

→ A modern young woman and a professional golfer
→ Friends with Daisy and Tom, involved with Nick
→ Jordan is fundamentally dishonest
→ Physically and in her mannerisms Jordan is a symbol of the young feminine ideal of the 1920s

George Wilson

→ A car mechanic whose wife is having an affair with Tom
→ Poor, ignorant and depressed
→ Misinformed by Tom, kills Gatsby and then takes his own life

Myrtle Wilson

→ George's wife, a sensual and coarse woman who cheats on her husband with Tom
→ Killed by Daisy who is driving a car Myrtle believes to be Tom's

Other persons: Meyer Wolfshiem, Dan Cody, Henry Gatz, "Owl Eyes", Michaelis, Catherine, Klipspringer and Pammy Buchanan.

Nick Carraway

Nick is a very interesting character to examine because of his **dual function in the book**. He is not only a character whose motivations and actions are relevant and must be examined, he is, as the narrator, the filter through which the entire story and everything in it must pass. Luckily for the reader, he is both non-judgemental (at least at the beginning; see the opening paragraph of the novel) and thoroughly honest (p. 84 ll. 13–15).

Decency and respect

At the opening of the novel Nick says that he was raised to remember that he has had many advantages in his life which other people haven't, and that he should therefore be careful in judging and criticising others (p. 5 ll. 2–7). Nick is conscientious, reserved and self-aware. He thinks about what he does, why he is doing it, and about the consequences of his actions for others: typically modestly, he says "I am slow thinking and full of interior rules that act on my desires", (p. 84 ll. 3–5), which makes him the only "adult" in the novel when compared to the childish and selfish search for pleasure and gratification which seems to motivate the other major characters.

Responsible behaviour

It is **important for Nick to behave correctly**. Daisy has heard that he is engaged to a girl back out west, which is not true (p. 32 ll. 14–27), but he nevertheless feels that he has to get himself "out of that tangle back home [...] there was a vague understanding that had to be tactfully broken off before I was free" (p. 84 ll. 6–12). This happens again when he feels that he must break off his connection to Jordan when he decides to leave and return to the Midwest – "There was one thing that had to be done before I left, an awkward, unpleasant thing that perhaps had better be let alone. But I wanted to leave things in order and not just trust that obliging and indifferent sea to sweep my refuse away" (p. 228 ll. 15–19). This behaviour is in stark contrast to the casual infidelity of Tom and Myrtle and Gatsby's sentimental, self-indulgent obsession with Daisy. Nick takes responsibility for his own actions, and when what he does affects another person, he feels he is responsible for that, too.

Ambivalent attitude towards life

By the end of the novel, however, despite what he says at the beginning, Nick *is* making judgements about the other characters. His dislike for Tom has been clear from the start but his disgust with his and Daisy's shallowness and cowardice is openly expressed (p.231 ll.14–20). Nick describes his attitude to life like this: "I was within and without, simultaneously enchanted and repelled by the inexhaustible variety of life" (p. 52 l. 26–p. 53 l. 2). This **ambivalence is one of the key elements** in the novel, where almost nothing is simple and merely what it seems to be. Nick is almost in love with Jordan, but he is at the same time aware that she is deeply dishonest and also very cold. He is fascinated by his cousin Daisy and falls under the spell of her sensuality, but he also knows that her attraction lies in her wealth. He comes to love Gatsby dearly ("You're worth the whole damn bunch put together", Nick says to him when they last see each other, p. 200 l. 15), but his dilemma is made clear when he says: "Gatsby represented everything for which I have an unaffected scorn" (p. 6 l. 17–p. 7 l. 1) and "I disapproved of him from beginning to end" (p. 200 ll. 17–18).

This dual ability to be attracted to and repelled by what he sees means that Nick is as skilled at evoking beauty and excitement, as he is writing about death, corruption and disillusionment. Although he is the narrator, and we the readers are closely bound to his character and his feelings about and reactions to the people and events, Nick is not always clear and direct. **His ambivalent feelings towards the major characters in the novel challenges the reader to think carefully.** He is telling a story that is for him two years old – at the beginning of the novel, Nick already knows everything that is going to happen – but the book nevertheless manages to chart his progress from his elated satisfaction to be spoken to as a resident of West Egg rather than a tourist (p. 9 ll. 17–25) to a disillusioned and disgusted man who goes back to where he came from, unable to bear being in the East any longer, where everything has "a quality of distortion" (p. 227 l. 22).

Jay Gatsby/James Gatz

The man called "Jay Gatsby" is the creation of the young James Gatz, son of a poor family in North Dakota. He dreamed of becoming wealthy and followed a rigorous schedule of self-improvement in order to become better and richer and cleverer than he felt himself to be. Gatz left home young to make his fortune and met a millionaire called Dan Cody, to whom he introduced himself as Jay Gatsby. He lived and worked with Cody until the old man's death but was left with nothing. He met and fell in love with a young woman called Daisy Fay, and was then sent to war, where he flourished and was awarded medals for bravery. During the war Daisy married Tom Buchanan. Later Gatsby met gambler and crook Meyer Wolfshiem, with whom he established a nationwide chain of drug stores through which they sold illicit alcohol. This business made him fabulously wealthy and he bought himself a huge mansion on Long Island, close to Daisy, where he lived until his murder at the end of the summer of 1922 at the age of "a year or two over thirty" (p. 69 ll. 26–7).

Gatsby's motivations

The key elements in Gatsby's mysterious nature are his unshakable and unscrupulous determination to improve himself, and his powerful and doomed desire to return to an illusory past. Both of these traits show his **obsession with the past** – whether escaping it or chasing it – and with optimistic hope. It is Gatsby's capacity for hope – and the wide-eyed, peculiarly innocent strength of his optimism and wonder – which inspires Nick's friendship and love. Despite the crime, corruption and deceit on which his life is based, Gatsby possesses a **childlike ability to dream**.

The most ambivalent character in a story rich with ambivalent, deceptive appearances, Gatsby has been interpreted as Fitzgerald's **symbol for America itself**: fabulously wealthy, generous, corrupt, possessing remarkable willpower and forever chasing a dream of a past which can never be regained.

Willpower

One of the most striking aspects of Gatsby's character is his extraordinary willpower, self-discipline and focus. Contrast the Buchanans, Daisy and Tom, with Gatz/Gatsby: the Buchanans are the classic idle rich, casually drifting on their wealth from Chicago to France and then to Long Island, enjoying all the luxuries and comforts and distractions their money can buy, not focussed on any particular goals. On the other side there is James Gatz/Jay Gatsby, who is shown to possess an iron will. After having seen what alcohol can do to a man (Dan Cody, see p. 136) he never drinks, but cynically builds his fortune on alcohol. His strict schedule for self-improvement, found by his father in an old book (pp. 223–224), exposes a young man who has identified a goal and will stop at nothing to achieve it. It should be remembered that this goal (becoming wealthier and less ignorant) pre-dates his **fixation on Daisy** – which only serves to reinforce the impression of a man who, once locked on to a target, will let nothing stop him from achieving it. In the process of developing from poor James Gatz to notoriously wealthy Jay Gatsby, he embodies the American Dream in its most extreme form.

Crime and notoriety

Gatz becomes a new man: changing his name, reinventing his past – a permanent theme in his life which will lead to his downfall – and fulfilling the **ideal of American freedom and independence**. This comes at a price, of course: his wealth is based on criminal activities (bootlegging and gambling). However pure his dreams may be, his methods are impure and stained by crime. He is followed by clouds of rumour and sinister theories about his origins and the source of his wealth. Nick describes these, and the unpleasant truth, as the "foul dust that floated in the wake of his dreams" (p. 7 l. 13). The rumours are initially "romantic speculation" (p. 64 l. 7), but become more threatening. A reporter appears, trying to investigate: Nick is introduced to Meyer Wolfshiem, an underworld figure who wears human teeth as cuff links: and Tom, having begun his own investigation into Gatsby's mysterious wealth, learns that a friend of his has ended up in jail for his involvement with Gatsby and Wolfshiem. Apparently, Gatsby is also involved in police corruption ("I was able to do the commissioner a favor once" p. 95 ll. 13–14).

These rumours and whisperings are all unimportant to him, as are the moral consequences of his business: all that matters is achieving the goal. The same is true of his infatuation with Daisy. He is very careful of her reputation – he arranges a meeting with her at Nick's house to maintain appearances, and fires all of his staff to avoid gossip, he claims – but everything else is meaningless to him. He only bought the mansion and began hosting the extravagant parties – "dispensing starlight to casual moths" (p. 109 ll. 22–23) – to be closer to Daisy. The fear that she didn't enjoy herself at his party depresses him (p. 148). Nothing is important except achieving his dreams – **wealth, status, Daisy**.

Gatsby's inner life

The importance he attaches to Daisy is linked to his youthful ambitions for wealth and status. **Gatsby's inner life is the mystery of the novel**, and it is only indirectly exposed: Jordan gives an account of his first meeting with Daisy, and he tells Nick a version of his own past which is full of half-truths before later telling him what seems to be the real, true story of how he met Daisy and how

James Gatz became Jay Gatsby, millionaire. What emerges from the combined stories is that Daisy was a beautiful and desirable American "princess", and that she and Gatsby fell in love shortly before he was shipped out to serve in the First World War. She was engaged to Tom Buchanan, who was from the same wealthy class as her family, but she almost, as Jordan tells Nick, calls off the wedding (see pp. 106–107) when she gets a letter from Gatsby. Gatsby's "failure" is that he was poor, that he came from a lower social class: that he had no money and no breeding. Everything that happens since meeting and falling in love with Daisy – which he also, in his own words, didn't expect to happen – is his attempt to change the past. He wants to make everything right for Daisy as she was then, in 1917, when they fell in love. His reckless bravery during the war, he tells Nick, came from not caring if he lived or died because of having lost Daisy. That crime and corruption are involved in his acquisition of wealth is equally irrelevant: all that matters is becoming the kind of man he wishes he had been when he and Daisy had first met (see pp. 149–150).

Trimalchio

Gatsby is identified with Trimalchio, both in Fitzgerald's original title for the novel and in a comment made by Nick (p. 151 l. 5). This reflects both Gatsby's past and the extravagant and showy uses he makes of his money. Trimalchio, a former slave who has been freed, became rich through hard work and perseverance. Once wealthy, he used his money to throw generous and excessive parties. The climax of the Classical Roman text is his funeral being acted out for his own amusement at one of his parties: this seems to have less relevance to Gatsby. Nick's comment is to say that his "career as Trimalchio" is finished – that it was a phase. The satirical relevance remains, however. No matter how wealthy he becomes or how popular, he will always be the **object of suspicion**

or rumour, and always on the wrong side of the invisible boundary which separates the upper and lower classes.

Daisy Buchanan

Significance of her name

The most immediate aspect of Daisy as a literary character is her name, which evokes a **delicate white flower**, and is contrasted with her husband's mistress Myrtle, also a plant name, that of a common shrub. Daisy's maiden name is Fay (p. 104 l. 6) – the old English word *fey* means fairy, but is also an adjective describing someone who is sensitive, mysterious and strange. The change in name from Fay to Buchanan – from the light monosyllable to the hard, clunky polysyllable – is significant. Daisy was originally a fairy-like creature, and then she became part of Tom's hard and very real world. And although she is most frequently described in terms of her airy, hypnotic beauty and the intense desire she awakens in men, there is now a bond between her and Tom which is impenetrable to outsiders.

Daisy's beauty

Gatsby's first impressions of her are that she is "excitingly desirable" (p. 193 l. 3) and has a "breathless intensity" (p. 193 l. 7). Nick's first sight of her after a long period with no contact is of an almost mystical figure in an airy, dreamlike space (see pp. 16–17): first there is a "rosy-colored space" which is described like a ship on the sea, billowing and airy, in subtle motion. The only stable and fixed object in the room is the couch Daisy and Jordan are lying on. The women are both dressed in white and are fluttering "as if they had just been blown back in after a short flight around the house". Daisy herself is "paralyzed with happiness", she says: she has a way of looking at someone, "promising that there was no one in the world she so much wanted to see". Nick is fascinated by her "low, thrilling" voice and by her "sad and lovely" face. He says that her voice has an excitement "men who had cared for her found difficult to forget" (p. 18 II. 20–21). She is subtly seductive, promising some undefined excitement and encouraging close, intense attention.

Her voice

The seductive, hypnotic quality of Daisy's voice is often mentioned. Nick reports that some people say that Daisy murmurs so softly "only to make people lean toward her" (p. 18 l. 4). Within just one scene (Chapter I, p. 25) Nick says her voice "compelled me forward breathlessly" and describes it as "glowing and singing" and "breathless, thrilling". Jordan later remarks on the seductive attraction of Daisy's voice (p. 108 ll. 12–13), and its Siren[16]-like qualities are suggested again in Chapter VI: "[...] as she said something low in his ear he turned toward her with a rush of emotion. I think that voice held him most with its fluctuating, feverish warmth because it couldn't be over-dreamed – that voice was a deathless song."

The satirical edge of Fitzgerald's writing later completely undercuts this mystical infatuation with Daisy's Siren-like voice. "Her voice is full of money", Gatsby says in Chapter VII (p. 161 l. 21). Nick acknowledges that this is true: "I'd never understood before. It was full of money – that was the inexhaustible charm that rose and fell in it" (p. 160 ll. 22–24).

Need for men

Her ability to seize male attention and hold it is important. Daisy seems to *need* men – or, more specifically, one man – who can protect and support her. **And the protection and support is not just love.** Gatsby's great appeal to her is not just his winning smile, good looks and intense adoration, but the lie that he is living: "he let her believe that he was a person from much the same strata as herself – that he was fully able to take care of her" (p. 194 ll. 6–8). What is meant here is of course money. Gatsby goes away to war,

---

16 In Greek mythology, the Sirens were deadly female sea creatures who lured sailors to their deaths with their beautiful voices.

leaving her with a broken heart, dreams of love, but no support and no husband. "She wanted her life shaped now, immediately – and the decision must be made by some force – of love, of money, of unquestionable practicality" (p. 197 ll. 4–7). Tom is this force. He may not bring the love – the nature of their relationship remains a mystery, of which more below – but pragmatically, he has money and power. And he belongs to the same social class. When she chooses him, while Gatsby is away in Europe, she feels "flattered [...] there was a certain struggle and a certain relief" (p. 197 ll. 11–12).

Daisy's choice

The central conflict of the novel is that Daisy must **choose between her old lover Jay Gatsby and her husband Tom Buchanan**. Her decision is influenced by many factors: love, security, excitement, comfort, submission to force. Tom understands much more quickly than Gatsby, who seems to never really grasp the fact that Daisy will never leave him and the security he offers. At the showdown in the hotel Tom treats Gatsby with "magnanimous scorn" (p. 178 l. 27).

Daisy and Tom's relationship is complicated. Nick, Jordan and Gatsby all see the evidence of a cruel and loveless connection, but right from the start there is a suggestion of the essential «otherness» of the two of them: "she looked at me with an absolute smirk on her lovely face as if she had asserted her membership in a rather distinguished secret society to which she and Tom belonged" (p. 29 ll. 21–24). This brief glimpse into their secret world is echoed twice again:

→ during the confrontation at the Plaza Hotel, Tom reminds Gatsby that "there're things between Daisy and me that you'll never know, things that neither of us can ever forget," (p. 176 ll. 6–8)

→ towards the end of the novel, when Nick peers in on them sitting in the kitchen after Daisy has killed Myrtle: "He was talking intently across the table at her and in his earnestness his hand had fallen upon and covered her own. Once in a while she looked up at him and nodded in agreement. They weren't happy [...] and yet they weren't unhappy either. There was an unmistakable air of natural intimacy [...] and anyone would have said that they were conspiring together." (p. 190 ll. 9–19)

The point which is perhaps reinforced here is that class divide which Gatsby feels so strongly, and which allows Tom and Daisy to separate themselves so coldly and callously from the trouble and pain they cause. As Gatsby observes, "Her voice is full of money" (p. 160 ll. 18–26), and Nick completely agrees. She is a "king's daughter, the golden girl" who lives in an artificial world, entirely protected on all sides by money, status and privilege.

Tom Buchanan

Uncomplicated

One of the least complex characters in the novel, Tom is physically powerful, wealthy, arrogant, domineering and violent. He is presented in an almost **exclusively negative light**. Fitzgerald portrays him as a racist bigot who feels contempt for anyone and everyone whom he considers to be socially beneath him. It becomes clear as the conflict between Gatsby and Tom escalates that he is not merely brutish and ignorant, but also cruel and vengeful – Gatsby is described as having broken against "Tom's hard malice" (p. 192 ll. 19–20). Tom is indirectly responsible for all three deaths in the novel. Fitzgerald is very unambiguous in his condemnation of Tom Buchanan, both in the language used to describe him and in his role in the events of the novel.

Blunt and ignorant

Tom is very literal – he seems to be immune to sarcasm or irony or subtlety. When Nick, during the dinner in Chapter I, casually mentions to Daisy that she is making him feel uncivilised, Tom begins a racist rant about the coming destruction of civilisation – of the white race – by the "other races" (pp. 23–24). Nick finds his **fixation on crude, racist theories** "pathetic" (p. 24 l. 16), and Daisy and Jordan also mock his racist anxieties: Daisy claims, when he asks what she and Nick have been talking about, that they had been discussing the Nordic race (p. 32 l. 4), making fun of his theories about the collapse of white civilisation. Later in the Plaza Hotel when he and Gatsby confront each other, Tom begins to rant about the decay of values and the threat of inter-racial marriage: Jordan sarcastically points out, "we're all white here" (p. 172 l. 24). Again, at the end of the book, when the terrible truth has emerged, Nick's feelings for Tom Buchanan become clear: "I felt suddenly as though I were talking to a child" (p. 231 ll. 21–22). This is the sum of Tom – a child with simple and selfish opinions and world view, whose careless violence and self-centred greed has caused the deaths of three people.

Fascination with apocalypse

Tom's ignorance is evident again when he becomes confused while trying to explain another apocalyptic theory – "the earth's going to fall into the sun – or wait a minute – it's just the opposite" (p. 157 ll. 11–12). He appears to be fascinated by the apocalypse, a detail in Fitzgerald's characterisation which further enriches the **atmosphere of violence, brutality and death** which surrounds him. On the first evening Nick is there he bruises Daisy's finger (p. 22 ll. 6–16). He has been involved in a car crash in which a young woman with whom he was apparently having an affair – a chamber maid from a hotel where he and Daisy were staying – broke her arm (p. 107 ll. 21–26). The language used to describe him is loaded with violent and brutish associations: Nick's first impression of him (Chapter I, pp. 14–16) includes the following words:

Adjectives used to describe Tom

hard – supercilious – arrogant – dominance – aggressively – enormous power – great pack of muscle – a cruel body – impression of fractiousness – contempt – stronger – harsh.

Pammy Buchanan

Child as object

Daisy's daughter is seldom mentioned, and only once by name. The only two significant moments in the novel relating to the child are when Daisy talks to Nick about her feelings at her birth, and later, when she introduces her to Gatsby. It is a further sign of **Daisy's vanity and self-centredness** that both these scenes are essentially about herself. Pammy is a possession to be paraded in front of Gatsby for his approval. The Buchanans are wealthy enough to have a nurse, so Daisy can have more time for herself and needn't exhaust herself looking after a child.

Because the novel is a social satire as well as being a tragic love story, Pammy highlights the **irresponsible and selfish behaviour of the people of the Jazz Age**, whose desire for fun, gratification and sensation consumes their attention, leaving them unable to properly care for those things which aren't fun or exciting – like their children.

Daisy only interested in her daughter as a reflection of herself

Pammy is first mentioned as "the baby" (p. 19 l. 11), and then only in passing. Nick later the same evening asks her about her daughter and Daisy eventually, obviously not interested in the subject, says "I suppose she talks, and – eats, and everything" (p. 28 l. 23). What interests her about her daughter is what she, Daisy, said at the birth: "I hope she'll be a fool – that's the best thing a girl can be in this world, a beautiful little fool" (p. 29 ll. 6–8). Nick notices the "basic insincerity" (p. 29 l. 17) of what she says, but aside from Daisy's insincerity, which is a major aspect of her character, we are seeing a woman whose only relationship to her own daughter is **how the child reflects on herself**.

When she is finally introduced in person (pp. 155–157) it is so that Daisy can display her to Gatsby and get her daughter's approval of "mother's friends". She is eager to dissociate Tom as much as possible from the product of her body when she introduces her to Gatsby. She is swiftly brought into the room and just as quickly swept away again, disappearing from the story.

Jordan Baker

Modern ideal

Jordan is, like Daisy, an extremely modern woman. She is a professional golfer and coolly cynical. Nick admires her "complete self sufficiency" (p. 18 l. 11) and is fascinated by her, a "clean, hard, limited person" (p. 110 l. 28) who is so much more direct and comprehensible than Daisy. She is often described as being "jaunty" (p. 72 l. 25, p. 83 l. 7, p. 110 l. 29, p. 229 l. 3), an adjective which means being confident and pleased with yourself.

Physically, she is almost **a stereotype of the fashionable feminine ideal of the 1920s**: "I enjoyed looking at her. She was a slender, small-breasted girl with an erect carriage which she accentuated by throwing her body backward at the shoulders like a young cadet" (p. 20 ll. 21–24). She is almost androgynous, and is built for sport and fun. Her excessively cool manner, at times scornful, sceptical or cynical, is equally typical of fashionable behaviour of the time. Jordan Baker is what was known as an "It girl": a woman whose looks, mannerisms and style captures the moment of an age, a snapshot of what is most desirable and admirable in a fashionable young woman.

But Fitzgerald's **treatment of the Jazz Age** is as always ambivalent, and Jordan's cool hard character is also unfortunately shallow and entirely self centred, reflecting the self-obsessed and brittle preoccupations of a generation which loses itself in irresponsibility and the quest for fun.

Dishonesty

Jordan is also explicitly identified as dishonest. So dishonest, in fact, that this is her defining characteristic. She is infamous for having cheated at a golf tournament, and Nick remembers this when the two of them begin to see each other more often during the summer. He grasps what it is her "bored haughty face" (p. 82 l. 6) is concealing: "She was incurably dishonest" (p. 83 l. 2).

She is, along with Gatsby himself and Michaelis, one of the main sources for the narrative: she tells Nick how Daisy and Gatsby first met in 1917 and how she came to marry Tom (pp.103–8). Nick appreciates her cool detachment (p. 111 ll. 10–15), so very different from Daisy's complex neediness and Myrtle's crudity. He sees her as being, in contrast to Daisy, "too wise ever to carry well-forgotten dreams from age to age" (p. 179 ll. 25–6). But, after the night when Daisy kills Myrtle, they talk on the phone and Nick is struck by her voice – no longer "fresh and cool" but "harsh and dry" (p. 201 ll. 11–15). Despite being "half in love" with her (p. 230 l. 1), Nick leaves her at the end, angry and disappointed by her **cold selfishness**.

Myrtle Wilson

Sensual, coarse and frustrated

Myrtle has been married to George Wilson for eleven years. She is in her mid-30s, and is therefore a little older than Tom, Nick, Gatsby and the other characters. She is "faintly stout" (p. 38 l. 16) but seems sensuous rather than overweight. The earthy **sexuality associated with Myrtle** is a stark contrast to the fairy-like elusive charm of Daisy: she is not beautiful ("no facet or gleam of beauty") but has a smouldering vitality (p. 38 ll. 19–21). Myrtle is dressed in a "spotted dress of dark blue" (p. 38 l. 18), very different again from the billowing pure white already associated with Daisy. Her voice is coarse where Daisy's is soft and glowing.

Myrtle and Daisy as opposites

Myrtle and Daisy are established as opposite forces from the beginning. Both have botanical names; both become involved in affairs with men other than their husbands; both are linked to Tom Buchanan; and both are desperate for male attention – so different from Jordan Baker or Myrtle's sister Catherine. The differences between the two women are extreme. Daisy is a wealthy upper class woman who was courted by many eligible young men, and Myrtle is a working class woman who has been married to a disappointing, unhappy man for eleven years. Myrtle, during the party she and Tom have in Chapter II, becomes increasingly affected, fake, and strained as she tries to play a role for which she is ill equipped. She provokes Tom by repeating Daisy's name until he slaps her, breaking her nose. Apparently she is also beaten by her husband: Michaelis is surprised she hasn't left him already.

Myrtle shares Gatsby's desire to be better, to be more than she is: but whereas his desire is given an almost mythical grandeur (his own Holy Grail) and is oddly non-materialistic, Myrtle's is really all about the luxury. She loves the toys, the dresses, the opulent furniture in the flat, the fact that Tom spoils her and buys her anything she wants.

Linked to Daisy in death

She is linked to Daisy by death as well. Daisy kills her by accident, we are told. Myrtle has mistaken Gatsby's car for Tom's (she had seen Tom driving the car earlier that day) and rushes out to stop the car, presumably to appeal to Tom to take her away after George, having learned of her infidelity (but not with whom), says he will take her away from New York. There is a **bitter irony** in Daisy being the one to kill Myrtle, her husband's mistress, using as a weapon the car belonging to her own lover. Myrtle's death so upsets George that, in his grief and rage, he murders Gatsby and then kills himself. Again, it is Tom who enables this tragedy.

George Wilson

Weak and oppressed

A pathetic and abused figure, George Wilson is at the mercy of his unfaithful wife and the irresistible force of Tom Buchanan's physical presence and wealth. He is **a weak and pale creature**, confined to the hellish "valley of ashes" and desperate for some kind of improvement. He badly wants to buy Tom's flashy car – they are constantly talking about it, as when we first see George in Chapter II (p. 38), when he calls at the Buchanans' (pp. 154–155), and when Tom drives past in Gatsby's yellow car (p. 164).

When George learns that Myrtle "had some sort of life apart from him in another world" (p. 165 ll. 5–6) he becomes physically sick. He is a weak, ghostly figure when on the day of the trip to New York and Myrtle's death. **Her death seems to break him**, and after a night of anguish he sets off to find and kill the man whom he believes to have killed Myrtle. He is pointed in the direction of Gatsby by Tom. He kills the wrong person and then himself, having been misled by Tom Buchanan.

Tom and George

Tom treats George with the contempt of a master for a servant. When Nick asks Tom whether George suspects that Myrtle is having an affair, Tom says "He's so dumb he doesn't know he's alive" (p. 40 l. 3). He seems to take a sadistic pleasure in making George beg for the car and threatens not to sell it to him (see p. 155 ll. 4–7). But as Nick realises when he sees the two men together, when it is clear that George has learned about Myrtle's infidelity, there is some strange bond between them. Both are being cheated on by their wives, but whereas **George's discovery makes him physically ill**, so "so sick that he looked guilty" (p. 165 l. 12), Tom still seems powerful and healthy.

The night after Myrtle's death

George is driven mad by grief the night of Myrtle's death and he sees the eyes of God in the billboard image of Dr T. J. Eckleburg (p. 207). He retreats into an impenetrable secret world of his own.

Michaelis, who is with him that night, can't reach him, and Nick, in telling the story, has to reconstruct his actions and movements based on what the police had learned and what witnesses had noticed. The final clue, the visit George makes to Tom, is something Nick only guesses until Tom confirms it.

George represents the world from which Gatsby/Gatz emerged: poverty, labour, hopelessness. They are clearly linked in death: the one who got away, who set his mind to making himself better, no matter the cost, and the other who lacked the energy and strength to drag himself out of the valley of ashes.

Meyer Wolfshiem, Mr Henry Gatz and Dan Cody

These are **the three fathers** of the complex man who calls himself Jay Gatsby.

- → The biological father, **Henry Gatz**, is a tired old man when we see him in the final chapter. In spite of his poor life in the Midwest, something the young James Gatz wanted to escape, he is proud of his son.
- → **Dan Cody**, his second father, was the inspiration he needed, the embodiment of his desires for wealth, independence, self-realisation – the American Dream.
- → Then there is **Meyer Wolfshiem**, his third father, who claims to have "made him" – who brought him into the underworld of gambling, bootlegging, smuggling, corruption and violence.

Henry Gatz

A ghost from the past

doesn't know who his son has become. He is proud of his accomplishments but also deceived about the nature of his business – he thinks Gatsby would have been a force for good, when he was in fact a criminal, a bootlegger (p. 217 ll. 22–23). He shows Nick the book in which young Jimmy Gatz had planned out his schedule (pp. 223–224) and seems very proud of it. But as quietly and quickly as he comes, he disappears again. Like a **ghostly reminder of the past**, Henry Gatz serves no purpose now: his son had left him and everything he represented and become someone completely different. Henry Gatz gives Gatsby life and something to escape from.

Dan Cody

Inspiration and mentor

gives Gatsby something to aspire to and the knowledge he will need **to climb the social ladder**. As his entire fortune is taken by a greedy wife, Gatsby is left with nothing but this knowledge when Cody dies. It was at their first meeting that James Gatz became Jay Gatsby (p. 133 ll. 5–16). Cody learns that Gatsby is quick-witted and ambitious and takes him along on his yacht. Nick describes a photo of Cody as showing a man with a "hard empty face – the pioneer debauchee who [...] brought back to the eastern seaboard the savage violence of the frontier brothel and saloon" (p. 136 l. 23–p. 137 l. 3). Another thing Gatsby learned from Cody was apparently sobriety. He saw too clearly **how awful drunken behaviour can be**.

Wolfshiem

Partner in crime

says to Nick of Gatsby, "I made him" (p. 221 l. 4). He had met Gatsby soon after he left the army, a decorated major who has no clothes, no money for food, and is desperate for a job (p. 220 ll. 21–28). He had seen immediately, as Cody had done, that Gatsby possessed certain traits which are very precious – his energy, his charm, his ambition. Between them they had managed to set up a very successful illegal alcohol smuggling operation. They bought drug stores all over the country and shipped alcohol to be sold illegally through these shops. Nick suspects that Gatsby might also have been involved in Wolfshiem's illegal gambling – he is supposed to have been responsible for "fixing", ie. manipulating, the 1919 baseball World's Series. Wolfshiem is friendly and hearty when Nick meets him, but **he is closely tied to the shadowy and sinister underworld of crime** – the first anecdote Nick hears him tell concerns the gunning down of a gangster by other gangsters, and at the same meal he proudly displays his cuff links, made from human teeth. He refuses to attend Gatsby's funeral, which disappoints Nick – the two of them were by all accounts quite close, not just as business partners.

"Owl Eyes"

Mysterious symbol of the Lost Generation

A very **ambiguous character** – we never learn his real name, for example – this man appears three times in person, and once as a ghostly suggestion. His presence and comments are loaded with implied significance from his first appearance in the library during one of Gatsby's parties, and his presence at the funeral also suggests that there is more to this figure.

Nick and Jordan first encounter him in the library at one of Gatsby's parties (p. 65). He is astounded, he says, that the books in the library are real. The implication is obviously that he expected them to be fake – to be merely decorative, examples of Gatsby's pretensions. This would be a fairly typical cliché of the uncultured *nouveau riche*: to surround themselves with the appearances of the upper classes, including well-stocked libraries. The owl-eyed man treats Gatsby's house and library like an extremely cleverly designed stage set. He takes a book from the shelf to show it to Jordan and Nick and then quickly replaces it, nervous that removing one element will cause the entire structure to collapse. This theatrical little episode strongly implies that **he believes that Gatsby's**

world is a lie, and that the entire edifice can easily come crumbling down. He emerges from this scene as a mysteriously remote figure who is wandering aimlessly, and whose view of the world is filtered through layers of irony and cynicism. The next time we see him only reinforces this opinion. Later that same evening, at the end of the party, he is involved in a slapstick car crash in Gatsby's driveway where he again seems to be **playing a role** for no particular audience, entertaining nobody except maybe himself with his misleadingly literal statements. His ghostly presence is felt later when Gatsby is showing his house to Daisy and Nick: "I could have sworn I heard the owl-eyed man break into ghostly laughter" when Gatsby closes the library doors (p. 124 ll. 12–13).

The strangeness of this character gives him a slightly sinister edge: there seems to be nothing innocent about his laughter and his wonder at Gatsby's surprisingly authentic books. He plays no real role in the action, he is simply **one of the many odd characters** Nick encounters during that summer and at Gatsby's parties. But, oddly, he is the only other person to attend Gatsby's funeral (pp. 225–226). Daisy, his great love, and Wolfshiem, his friend and partner, have both refused to come. But this strange man attends, and shares Nick's astonished dismay that none of the "hundreds" who enjoyed Gatsby's generosity could make the effort to come to his funeral. "The poor son-of-a-bitch", he says, before vanishing.

Michaelis and Catherine

George and Myrtle's supporting cast

These two characters are the Wilsons' supporting cast. **Catherine**, Myrtle's sister, is first encountered at the drunken party Tom and Myrtle have in New York. The next time she is mentioned it is after Gatsby's death and Nick is compelled to reassess her in a more positive light. Her refusal to drag her sister into a mess of speculation about infidelity and jealous murder does her credit (p. 211).

Michaelis is the source of much of the information Nick, and therefore we as readers, have about George Wilson. We learn very little about him: he is Greek, he owns a coffee shop near the "valley of ashes", and he is a loyal and compassionate friend to George, being the only one to stay with him through the terrible night following Myrtle's death. He is not stupid and has seen perfectly clearly how unhappy the Wilsons are together, and he thinks that Myrtle running into the road may have been just as much running away from George as running to another man.

Other characters: Klipspringer, the servants, party guests etc.

The parasites and party people

Ewing Klipspringer, the "boarder" (p. 87 ll. 5–7), is a symbol of the parasitic nature of the crowds who gather around Gatsby's generosity. He is at Gatsby's house so often, enjoying the free food and alcohol and a place to stay, that Nick is sure he has no home of his own. Gatsby doesn't seem to object to him being around all the time, and he asks him to play the piano for Daisy and Nick while he is showing them around his house (pp. 124–130). But when it comes to the funeral arrangements, Klipspringer is as evasive and disinterested as are all the others: he calls to get back some tennis shoes, making the excuse that he won't be able to attend the funeral because he's been invited to go on a picnic (p. 218 ll. 3–p. 219 l. 4). Nick is disgusted and hangs up in mid-sentence, appalled at the shallowness and dishonesty of the crowd who had nourished themselves on Gatsby's wealth.

There are **several servants** who pass through the story, leaving little or no impression. Gatsby's efficient butler is replaced by Wolfshiem's shady relatives when Daisy starts to come to the house. Some of the servants attend the funeral.

The party guests range from the delightful to the freakish. There are identical twins in matching dresses, grossly drunken people, movie stars and producers, and the whole list given in Chapter IV (pp. 85–88). The guests are usually not invited: they simply turn up and enjoy Gatsby's hospitality. They represent the **wild party-loving crowds of the Jazz Age**, the drinking, dancing, music-loving generation who are trying to evade responsibility and pursue fun with no consequences.

3.5 Notes on Themes

There are a number of themes in *The Great Gatsby* which Fitzgerald handles using various situations and characters. These themes are mostly universal, although some are very specific to the world of the novel – to the Jazz Age, and to the USA. The major themes and associated issues are:

→ America and the American Dream
→ Society and wealth
→ The Jazz Age: the modern world
→ Desire and the past
→ Vision.

America and the American Dream

The American Dream embodies two conflicting yet inseparable elements: the triumph of the human spirit and will, and an obsession with material wealth. Nick admires the former in Gatsby, and it seems that it is only in Gatsby that these qualities can be found: only he has the hope, the purity of intention, and the ability to dream. But Gatsby is corrupted. He is neither fully good nor wholly bad. While his motivations, will power and strength of character are admirable, his methods and means are highly questionable. He becomes rich by feeding off society's addiction to alcohol and gambling.

TEXT	REFERENCE	ANALYSIS
The truth was that Jay Gatsby, of West Egg, Long Island, sprang from his Platonic conception of himself. […] he invented just the sort of Jay Gatsby that a seventeen year old boy would be likely to invent, and to this conception he was faithful to the end.	p. 133 ll. 8–16	Nick describes James Gatz' creation of Gatsby as being an act of Platonic conception (p. 133 ll. 9–10), which refers to the Greek philosopher Plato's theory of there being "ideal" forms above and beyond the changing material, physical forms. This reference expresses the idea that Gatsby created the ideal version of himself – ideal here also meaning, thanks to the link to Plato, not only "best" but also permanent, unchanging. This is a development of the American Dream ideal of self-improvement
[The schedule]	p. 223 l. 8–p. 224 l. 15	Young James Gatz sets himself a strict schedule for self-improvement, a personal American Dream.
"I wouldn't ask too much of her", I ventured. "You can't repeat the past." "Can't repeat the past?" he cried incredulously. "Why of course you can!" He looked around him wildly as if the past were […] just out of reach of his hand. "I'm going to fix everything just the way it was before […]"	p. 149 ll. 4–11	In the ideal version of himself he has created, wealthy, successful Jay Gatsby is frozen in time, a perfect unchanging figure who is supposed to seize a dream of the past and hold it. This self-creation is an extreme form of the self-realisation, the freedom to succeed, which is essential to the American Dream.

American identities

The theme of America and American society is also dealt with in the book. For Nick, there is a **big difference between the West and the East**. The East – specifically New York in the novel – is characterised as a place of modernity, mass culture, a faintly surreal world where morals and codes of behaviour are fluid. A familiar theme in the literature of the USA has always been the relationship to the "Old World" to Europe, a theme most thoroughly examined by Henry James[17] in novels like *The Portrait of a Lady*. The idea that there was a freshness and innocence to the young American culture, the New World, which was in danger of being corrupted by contact with the old world, can be seen here in Nick's experience of the East, which is the region most closely identified with European culture and society (especially the big coastal cities like Boston and New York).

TEXT	REFERENCE	ANALYSIS
I see now that this has been a story of the West, after all – Tom and Gatsby, Daisy and Jordan and I, were all Westerners, and perhaps we possessed some deficiency in common which made us subtly unadaptable to Eastern life.	p. 227 ll. 12–16	Nick's recollection of his childhood is coloured by nostalgia and the love for familiar, comforting things: this, and his feeling that he and the other characters were unsuited to the East, reflects the novel's preoccupation with the lost things of the past.

17 1843–1916 American novelist, author of novels including *The Portrait of a Lady, The Golden Bowl, The Wings of the Dove, The Bostonians* and *The Europeans*. James was a literary realist, and his major theme was encounters between Americans and Europe. As a writer he made extensive use of detailed inner monologues to explore consciousness and perception

TEXT	REFERENCE	ANALYSIS
[The distorted dream of the East]	p. 227 l. 22–p. 228 l. 9	The dream shows how disturbed Nick is by the anonymity and callousness of the East – the debauchery which can lead to such loss of control, the casual way a nameless helpless woman can be carried around and disposed of by strangers. It resonates with echoes of the novel: of the parties, the drunkenness at Myrtle's party as well as at Gatsby's gatherings, the way men treat women so casually (contrast this with Nick's own very delicate behaviour towards women), the anonymity of the city when compared with the familiar, homely world of the West.

American values

Nick and Gatsby both embody certain American values which have become eroded and are no longer relevant in the East. They both come from the Midwest, what is sometimes called the "heartland" of America, **the home of traditional values and structures and way of life**. Nick's refined upbringing, with its careful attention to the feelings of others is contrasted with Gatsby's combination of original American idealism and the influence of the pioneer adventurer Dan Cody. Their origins are obviously not able to prepare the two men for the world of the East coast, as both fail – Gatsby is murdered and Nick returns home.

TEXT	REFERENCE	ANALYSIS
In my younger and more vulnerable years my father gave me some advice that I've been turning over in my mind ever since. "Whenever you feel like criticizing anyone," he told me, "just remember that all the people in this world haven't had the advantages that you've had."	p.5 ll.2-7	Nick comes from a refined family whose awareness of their position makes them treat people around them with delicacy and care.
Cody was fifty years old then, a product of the Nevada silver fields, of the Yukon, of every rush for metal since Seventy-five. […] the pioneer debauchee who during one phase of American life brought back to the eastern seaboard the savage violence of the frontier brothel and saloon.	p. 135 ll. 7–9, p. 137 ll. 1–3	Gatsby's origins are inspired by a proto-capitalist wild man from the frontier. His taste is inspired by the gaudy ostentation of a successful adventurer.

TEXT	REFERENCE	ANALYSIS
[...] for a transitory enchanted moment man must have held his breath in the presence of this continent, compelled into an aesthetic contemplation he neither understood nor desired, face to face for the last time in history with something commensurate to his capacity for wonder.	p. 233 ll. 6–11	This sense of wonder echoes Gatsby's nature – his encountering for the last time something to which it is equal. With this short but complex passage, Fitzgerald has Nick comment on the sadness and eventual futility of dreams and desires: the settlement of America was the last moment in history when the human capacity for wonder met with something big, strange and new enough to be able to promise to fulfil that sense of wonder. What came of those first dreams is American history, and in the novel, is reflected in the corruption of Gatsby's energy and dreams.

Society and wealth

The materialism of the American Dream is further complicated by the new era of consumerism and mass culture which the 20th century brought. Wealth and poverty (Tom and George) and class differences (Daisy and Gatsby) are powerful themes in the novel and are linked to the theme of deceptive appearances.

The exclusiveness of the wealthy classes

The idea of status and wealth providing exclusiveness, of an elite group, is very important for Gatsby and Daisy. Gatsby knew when they met that he was an impostor, and Tom is contemptuous of Gatsby's "new money", assuming – rightly, as it turns out – that it was made from bootlegging. However wealthy **Gatsby** may become he **will never really be a member of the exclusive club** to which Tom, Daisy and even Nick belong. He can't fool the "real" upper class any more than Myrtle can fool anyone with her grotesque behaviour at the party in her flat in Chapter II. Tom and Daisy's relationship is exclusive for this reason as well as for the strange nature of their love for one another. Tom can obviously offer Daisy something more than money – Gatsby has money – and an exciting, fun-filled life – Gatsby has proved that he can throw legendary parties. **There is a coarseness to the world of new money** and West Egg which Daisy finds distasteful. She enjoys being adored by him, but not the drunkenness and hysterical crowds at his parties. There is a self-protecting and elusive aura about the privileged classes which cannot be compensated for with money alone.

Beneath the appearances however there is a fairly straightforward fact: **old money**, as represented by Daisy and Tom, is callous, selfish, careless, brutal in its treatment of other people (consider especially Tom's treatment of George Wilson). **New money**, symbolised by Gatsby, is, for all its faults, generous and happy and eager to meet the world and make friends with it. This satirical treatment of the theme by Fitzgerald highlights his disapproval of the exclusive elites without overly praising the fresh and energetic modern world.

The treatment of wealth and money in the novel adds a satirical edge to an old cliché: Gatsby literally tries to buy happiness – and fails.

TEXT	REFERENCE	ANALYSIS
[…] what foul dust floated in the wake of his dreams […]	p. 7 l. 13	The origins of Gatsby's wealth and ambitions are corrupted by crime and crass materialism, as is he himself.

TEXT	REFERENCE	ANALYSIS
"He threw dust into your eyes."	p. 231 l. 2	Tom thinks that Gatsby deliberately lied to and tricked people, especially Daisy and Nick.
He might have despised himself, for he had certainly taken her under false pretenses [...] he had deliberately given Daisy a sense of security; he let her believe that he was a person from much the same strata as herself.	p. 194 ll. 3–8	Gatsby knew when he met Daisy that he was an impostor and that she came from a different world.
Gatsby looked at me questioningly. He wanted to go and he didn't see that Mr. Sloane had determined that he shouldn't. [...] "My God, I believe the man's coming," said Tom. "Doesn't he know she doesn't want him?"	p. 140 ll. 3–5 and 18–19	Tom and some snobbish friends of his turn up at Gatsby's house and the class divide becomes embarrassingly obvious, with Gatsby trying to be nice and clearly not understanding the nuances of upper class contempt.
Americans, while occasionally willing to be serfs, have always been obstinate about being peasantry.	p. 121 ll. 6–8	Nick's satirical comment means that while Americans have been willing to be serfs (that is, to work slavishly hard) they don't like to acknowledge their inferiority to wealth and power.

TEXT	REFERENCE	ANALYSIS
Gatsby was overwhelmingly aware of the youth and mystery that wealth imprisons and preserves […] and of Daisy, gleaming like silver, safe and proud above the hot struggles of the poor.	p. 195 ll. 6–7	This insight of Gatsby's expresses the enormous privilege of wealth, the escape it provides from the heat and struggle of not having enough money (one of James Gatz' most important motivations) and the division of society: the wealthy classes see themselves, and are seen by others, as being apart from the rest of humanity. This theme is apparent from the beginning with Nick's father reminding him that not everyone has the advantages of coming from a respected and wealthy family.
"Nowadays people begin by sneering at family life and family institutions and next they'll throw everything overboard and have intermarriage between black and white."	p. 172 ll. 15–21	Tom, as the voice of traditional class values, is betraying his hypocrisy (his affair with Myrtle and complete disinterest in his own child). He links a traditionalist stance with bigoted opinions about race.
"A lot of these newly-rich people are just big bootleggers, you know."	p. 146 ll. 8–9	Tom's "old money" suspicion of Gatsby's origins have inadvertently touched on the truth.
They were careless people, Tom and Daisy – they smashed up things and creatures and then retreated back into their money or their vast carelessness or whatever it was that kept them together […]	p. 231 ll. 15–19	Nick condemns the arrogance and selfishness with which the Buchanans, representing powerful "Old Money", treat the world around them, like thoughtless and irresponsible children.

The Jazz Age

Hedonism

The modern world of *The Great Gatsby* is the Jazz Age, **the age of flappers, cars, dancing and music**. The crowds at Gatsby's parties represent this generation, and Daisy was a flapper when she was younger. This lifestyle is associated with sexual liberty and plenty of alcohol, dancing and music. Neither Daisy nor Gatsby drink: he saw what it did to Dan Cody, and Daisy, Jordan suggests, doesn't drink because she likes to stay clear-headed while others around her lose control. Daisy is appalled by the crowds at Gatsby's parties: this manifestation of the Jazz Age is not like her own wealthy world of pleasure.

Literary use of intoxication

The intoxicating, disorientating effects of alcohol are used as a literary device in the novel, illustrating how much it can alter behaviour and consciousness: Myrtle's party (Chapter II) is an increasingly incoherent, distorted blur as Nick – and his narration – fades in and out of focus. This disturbing episode is contrasted with the exciting fun of Gatsby's summer parties. They capture a brief moment in time, an impression Fitzgerald had of the good things about the Jazz Age, that it had been a brief moment of wild youth. He writes in the essay *Echoes of the Jazz Age* that "it was borrowed time anyway – the whole upper tenth of a nation living with the insouciance of grand dukes and the casualness of chorus girls"[18].

---

18 http://fitzgerald.narod.ru/crackup/056e-eho.htm

TEXT	REFERENCE	ANALYSIS
"I never care what I do, so I always have a good time."	p. 62 ll. 29–30	The crowds at Gatsby's parties represent the careless hedonism of the Jazz Age.
...he dispensed starlight to casual moths...	p. 109 ll. 22–23	Gatsby's parties are fleeting events designed to attract Daisy's attention: desire is the motivation. The crowds who gather are fluttering and irrelevant, attracted to the light and warmth of his love. He doesn't give the parties for them, really, and they are not there for him. This brief phrase illustrates the hollowness and impersonality of the hedonism of the age.
They moved with a fast crowd, all of them young and rich and wild, but she came out with an absolutely perfect reputation. Perhaps because she doesn't drink. It's a great advantage not to drink among hard drinking people.	p. 108 ll. 5–9	Daisy belonged to a wealthy class of "flapper" when she was younger. The fact that she doesn't drink suggests that, under the surface, she has very careful control of herself and her environment. This impression is a bitter comment on the contrast of her love for Gatsby as an adventure with his love for her as a life-determining obsession.

TEXT	REFERENCE	ANALYSIS
[…] everything that happens has a dim hazy cast over it […] the whiskey distorted things […] it was nine o'clock – almost immediately afterwards I looked at my watch and found it was ten […] ...I was standing beside his bed and he was sitting up between the sheets, clad in his underwear […] Then I was lying half asleep in the cold lower level of the Pennsylvania Station […]	Chapter II pp. 43–56	Myrtle's party is a strange and disorientating affair where time slips and people change dramatically. Myrtle changes clothes and her character changes as she becomes increasingly fake and grotesque. The people at the party are self-centred and seem incapable of actually communicating with one another. Nick wants to leave but can't – he feels restrained. There is no joy in this chapter, just intoxication and a burst of violence when Tom breaks Myrtle's nose. Nick's grip on the narration seems to slip in this chapter as he tries to convey the confusion and unreality of the night.
I was enjoying myself now. I had taken two finger bowls of champagne and the scene had changed before my eyes into something significant, elemental and profound.	p. 68 ll. 8–10	The contrast to the unpleasant drunkenness at Myrtle's party in the previous chapter could not be stronger. Gatsby's gatherings, inspired by love, create for a single summer a wonderfully enchanting sense of being more than they are. The illusion is magical and temporary.

Telephones and cars

The satirical treatment of the modern age and its culture and toys can be seen in the significance placed on two, at the time, exciting innovations: **telephones and cars**.

Telephone calls in the novel are almost invariably linked with crime (Gatsby) or infidelity (Tom, Myrtle). Gatsby receives numerous mysterious phone calls throughout the novel, all of which are suggestively linked to his sinister business. This is confirmed later, after Gatsby's death, with the telephone call from Slagle. Tom is also connected to telephone calls of a mysterious and illicit nature: in his case it has to do with Myrtle or with George – with his infidelity or with his cruel domination. **The telephone is thus clearly identified with crime and immorality**. When Gatsby dies telephones become practically useless (pp. 212–213): Nick can't reach the people he is trying to contact. It is as if the telephones have failed or fallen silent with his death.

TELEPHONE CONVERSATION	REFERENCE	ANALYSIS
Chicago	p. 70 l. 2	The telephone calls Gatsby receives throughout the novel acquire an increasingly mysterious and sinister feel: this impression is confirmed after his death by the call Nick takes from Slagle, which is about some trouble with Gatsby's gambling and betting manipulation business. The telephone is a means for Gatsby to run his nation wide illegal operations. The convergence of extremely modern technology and modern criminal enterprise points up both the corrupt energy within modern American reality – despite Prohibition, Americans want to drink, and will support a criminal industry which makes that possible – and the function of mass culture (here evident in the technology of telephones) is enabling this corruption.
Philadelphia	p. 76. l. 8	
Detroit	p. 202 ll. 11–14	
"He has to telephone," said Mr. Wolfshiem, following him with his eyes.	p. 100 ll. 7–10	
"...I can't talk now... I said a *small* town ... Well he's no use to us if Detroit is his idea of a small town..."	p. 128 ll. 9–15)	
Gatsby had been called to the phone [...]	p. 144 l. 2	
[The telephone call from Slagle]	p. 215 ll. 1–19	

TELEPHONE CONVERSATION	REFERENCE	ANALYSIS
"Tom's got some woman in New York." "Got some woman?" I repeated blankly. "She might have the decency not to telephone him at dinner-time."	p. 24 l. 18–p. 26 l. 19	Considering Tom's role as the indirect agent of the deaths in the novel involving the unfortunate Wilsons, these secretive telephone conversations acquire an even greater significance. Just as Gatsby's business is facilitated by the technology of long-distance telephone conversations, and his criminal enterprises feed the appetites of the time, so is Tom and Myrtle's infidelity symbolic of the sexual liberties and immoralities of the age.
The telephone rang inside, startlingly, and as Daisy shook her head decisively at Tom [...] I was conscious of wanting to look squarely at everyone and yet to avoid all eyes.	p. 27 ll. 10–23	
"The rumor is," whispered Jordan, "that that's Tom's girl on the telephone." We were silent. The voice in the hall rose high with annoyance. "Very well then, I won't sell you the car at all..."	p. 154 l. 24–p. 155 l. 10	

Cars: death and desire

Even more explicitly than telephones, cars are identified with both the **freedoms and pleasures of the modern age**, and with death and violence. **Cars** are probably the most potent and extensively used symbol in the novel to represent both death and desire. As status symbols they are objects of desire. They define their owners as being modern, wealthy, free, energetic: they allow their owners to share their characteristics, they reflect on their owners.

CHARACTER / CAR	REFERENCE	ANALYSIS
Gatsby and his yellow station wagon: the car as status symbol	p. 56 l. 16 p. 88 l. 15 p. 89 ll. 8–17 p. 161 ll. 21–22	Like his over-the-top mansion, Gatsby's car is also wildly extravagant: it is at first a cheerful, busy sight: it "scampered like a brisk yellow bug" to pick up his party guests: when Nick sees it he describes it as "gorgeous"; sitting in it feels like being in a moving living room. Tom, in a mixture of envy and recognition of Gatsby's gaudy and showy lack of taste, calls it a "circus wagon". Gatsby has the money to buy an excessively showy status symbol, but lacks the taste of the upper classes. Like his parties, it is fun and flashy and entertaining and symbolic of the new money and new desires of a modern generation.
Daisy: cars and desire	p. 193 ll. 10–15 p. 193 l .3 p. 198 l. 18	When Gatsby tells Nick about his history with Daisy, cars become firmly associated with desire: her beautiful house has "a hint of [...] romances that were [...] redolent of this year's shining motor cars" and the cars, like her house, acquire the "breathless intensity" Gatsby connects with Daisy. Cars are for Gatsby as "excitingly desirable" as Daisy herself, because they are also fresh, exciting, new and promise a better world. Daisy herself, in the same memory, is again associated with the colour white ("in her white car").

CHARACTER / CAR	REFERENCE	ANALYSIS
George and Tom's car: desire and freedom	p. 38 ll. 1–11 p. 164 l. 3–p. 165 l. 16 p. 155 ll. 1–10	George Wilson's desperate desire for Tom's car makes this connection between cars and freedom very clear – Wilson wants to have Tom's car so that he can work on it and sell it, and so that he can take Myrtle out West to start a new life. He asks Tom about it both times we see them together, and calls to ask about it on the day Myrtle dies. Tom takes pity on George and agrees to sell him the car when he realises that Myrtle's affair has been discovered. The freedom George is seeking is like the dream Gatsby chases: it is an elusive, illusory promise which can never be achieved.
The death car	p. 107 ll. 21–26 p. 181 l. 14 p. 96 ll. 1–7	Tom's association with cars as symbols of death and desire began in the past. Jordan tells Nick about his marriage to Daisy, and about how soon after the honeymoon he had been involved in a car crash in which a young woman – a chambermaid from the hotel where he and Daisy had been staying – had been injured. Jordan doesn't comment further but it is clear that Tom had been having an affair with the woman. The car as a symbol closely connected with desire and death has already been firmly established by the time Daisy, driving madly in her lover's "gorgeous" car, runs over her husband's mistress. The yellow car, so admired

CHARACTER / CAR	REFERENCE	ANALYSIS
		by Nick and of which Gatsby is so proud, has become the "death car", coming out of the "gathering darkness" to kill Myrtle and then disappear. The yellow car has also been linked to death when it becomes part of a funeral procession in Chapter IV. The car becomes a symbol of a corrupted culture of materialism and the desire for status symbols: Gatsby's car, the most extravagant of them all, becomes an instrument of death, and its very uniqueness makes it that much easier for George, guided by Tom, to find him and kill him.
Good and bad drivers: Driving as metaphor for personality	p. 83 l. 8–p. 84 l. 15 p. 229 ll. 17–27	There are two other connected episodes involving cars approached from another angle: Nick accuses Jordan of being a terrible driver, and she doesn't take him seriously. "It takes two to make an accident" she says. Her carelessness as a driver, she says, is balanced out by other peoples' care. This, she says, is why she likes Nick. Later, when they are breaking up, she accuses him of being "another bad driver" – this is untrue and unfair, but what Jordan is saying can be read as a reflection on Daisy and Myrtle – two "bad drivers", careless women, and Jordan's comment that it takes two to make an accident is given weight by Myrtle running into the car to escape, either from George or to Tom.

Desire and the past

Desire is the greatest motivator in the novel: Gatsby's desire for Daisy is described by Nick as having "colossal vitality" (p. 131 ll. 1–2). Gatsby wants to be rich, he wants Daisy, Daisy wants both Gatsby and the security of Tom, Tom wants Daisy and Myrtle, Myrtle wants Tom, George wants the car, Wolfshiem wants to make money, and the crowds at Gatsby's parties want to have fun.

What Nick finally understands, as he is getting ready to return home to the Midwest, is that in choosing to pursue dreams and desires of the past into the future we are constantly moving backwards. Nostalgia – the sentimental desire for the past – is a poison and a handicap, Nick understands. All these characters who are around the age of 30 in that summer of 1922 **are struggling to hold on to the desires of their younger selves**. Their fear of the future only makes things worse, Fitzgerald seems to be suggesting: when they choose, as Gatsby did, to obsess about the past, then they and their dreams are doomed.

DESIRE…	REFERENCE	ANALYSIS
For Daisy	Gatsby found her "excitingly desirable" (p. 193 l. 3) Daisy's voice: p. 18 l. 4, ll. 13–24	Daisy is a potent symbol of the power of desire. She is described by Nick as a desirable woman and it is Gatsby's passion for her that drives the plot. The repeated references to the beauty and seductive nature of her voice, described as a "deathless song", suggests very strongly that she is like the Sirens of Greek mythology, beautiful women whose enchanting song seduced sailors to their deaths.

DESIRE...	REFERENCE	ANALYSIS
Corrupted	Daisy's desire for Gatsby, Myrtle's for Tom and George's for Tom's car bring disappointment Myrtle's desire for Tom and Gatsby's for Daisy bring death	Both Daisy and Gatsby's car are objects of desire that become associated with death. The world Fitzgerald describes is so corrupted that merely *wanting* something brings anything from disappointment and suffering (Daisy's desire for Gatsby, George's desire for Tom's car) to death (Gatsby's desire for Daisy, Myrtle's desire for Tom). This world is shown to be a hard and complex place where the ability to dream and hope is punished: where people seize gratification and immediate pleasure.
Dreams of the past	Jordan: p. 179 ll. 25–26 The green light: p. 34 ll. 12–20, p. 127 ll. 14–20 , p. 233 ll. 12–20 Gatsby's doomed obsession with the past: p. 149 l. 11 p. 178 l. 16 p. 199 ll. 10–12	Jordan, the most cynical and "modern" character in the book, is described by Nick as being "too wise ever to carry well-forgotten dreams from age to age". Gatsby is trying to recreate the past in order to capture the dreams of a younger time. He reaches out for the green light of Daisy's pier across the water from where he lives. A symbol Nick later interprets as being the "orgastic future that year by year recedes before us". It represents for him, and for Gatsby, the dreams of the past. When he and Daisy are reunited in Chapter V he tells her how important the green light was for him. It becomes clear to him that "the colossal significance of that light had now vanished forever [...] Now it was again a green

DESIRE...	REFERENCE	ANALYSIS
		light on a dock. His count of enchanted objects had diminished by one". The lesson here, which Gatsby seems to sense but not understand, is that dreams are only powerful for as long as they are out of reach. He believes he can recreate the past ("I'm going to fix everything just the way it was before"). His dream dies in the confrontation with Tom in the Plaza hotel ("only the dead dream fought on") but he seems not to want to accept this, lurking outside Tom's house to guard over Daisy. It is only much later, after Daisy has killed Myrtle and returned to Tom, that Nick thinks Gatsby has understood that he has lost the dream: "It was all going by too fast now for his blurred eyes and he knew that he had lost that part of it, the freshest and the best, forever".

Vision

Eyes and the act of seeing play an important role in this novel in which appearances can be so deceptive. The most striking example of this is the billboard overlooking the valley of ashes, the "persistent stare" of the disembodied eyes of Doctor T. J. Eckleburg.

The huge advertisement is one of the most powerful images in the novel, suggesting yet another presence – besides the author (Fitzgerald) and the narrator (Nick) – who is observing and judging the characters and the world.

Focus and perception

The act of seeing involves adjusting vision; to focus on something close, or to draw back and take in the bigger picture. Nick, as the narrator, is constantly refocussing, from the intimate details of small gatherings (his first evening at Tom and Daisy's house, Myrtle's little party, the overheated confrontation in the Plaza) to the broader scale of life on the East coast, the landscape of the valley of ashes, the panorama of Gatsby's huge parties, meditations on human nature and the futile pursuit of dreams.

THE EYES	REFERENCE	ANALYSIS
Dr. T. J. Eckleburg	p. 37 l. 6 p. 39 ll. 22–23 p. 163 ll. 11–12 p. 165 l. 21 p. 207 ll. 10–20	These disembodied eyes are so prominent that it is no surprise when they are later compared to the eyes of God. They look out over the lifeless, hellish place where the Wilsons live. Tom is seen "exchanging a frown" with these eyes while commenting on how terrible the place is. This short exchange suggests a kinship between these two figures, both of whom have such incredible dominance over George Wilson – Tom, who dominates him physically and financially and who has also "taken" his wife: and Dr. Eckleburg, whose giant eyes dominate the landscape and spiritual hell of George Wilson's life. During his terrible night after Myrtle's death, George appeals to the eyes on the billboard as if they were the eyes of God. He says he told Myrtle "she

THE EYES	REFERENCE	ANALYSIS
		couldn't fool God – I took her to the window […] and I said 'God knows what you've been doing' […] Michaelis saw with a shock that he was looking at the eyes of Doctor T. J. Eckleburg". The giant eyes are a constant presence: Fitzgerald reminds us of them whenever the action of the novel passes through the valley of ashes. When the central characters take their trip to the city in Chapter VII, a glimpse of the eyes reminds Nick of "Gatsby's caution about gasoline" – this is another sinister push towards his doom. Gatsby's well-intentioned warning to Tom leads to his yellow car, driven by Tom, being seen at Wilson's garage on the day of Myrtle's death.
Nick	p. 10 l. 16– p. 11 l. 2 p. 141 ll. 19–22 p. 228 ll. 10–11	Nick describes his vision as "limited" when he says that he had become "well-rounded": "life is much more successfully looked at from a single window, after all". This is perhaps an example of the narrator being overly modest, as Nick is not only careful with his judgements and criticisms, but is also very understanding of other peoples' weaknesses and attitudes.

THE EYES	REFERENCE	ANALYSIS
		When Nick sees Gatsby's world "through Daisy's eyes" he is disappointed: "It is invariably saddening to look through new eyes at things upon which you have expended your own powers of adjustment". This brief observation again highlights Nick's interesting role as character and narrator: his perspective – and therefore his narrative – is affected by his interpretation of another character's reaction to what they are both seeing.
		So much of the novel is concerned with appearances and with their deceptive nature that it is also relevant when Nick says, towards the end, that after Gatsby's death the East became "haunted [...] distorted beyond my eyes' power of correction". Perception is all-important: the events of 1922 have so altered Nick's perception that he can no longer look at the world of the East Coast without thinking of the corruption underlying the wealthy, flashy surfaces.

THE EYES	REFERENCE	ANALYSIS
Gatsby	p. 125 ll. 6–8 p. 148 ll. 7	Gatsby's vision is tragically determined by what he thinks other people want to see. He becomes rich because he thinks Daisy will love him if he can show her the appearance of wealth. When she signals dislike for the world he has created with his parties at the mansion then he immediately dismisses everything. The superficial nature of the world he has made is commented on by Owl Eyes in the library, who is astonished that the books are real. Nick observes him: "He hadn't once ceased looking at Daisy and I think he revalued everything in his house according to the measure of response it drew from her well-loved eyes."
Tom	p. 14 l. 20 p. 142 l. 12	Tom's eyes are twice described as "arrogant", contributing to Fitzgerald's unusually unambiguous characterisation. Tom sees the world in a very simple way, much simpler than George, Gatsby or Nick.

3.6 Style and Language

Because Fitzgerald uses a narrator who is himself a character within the novel, he can make use of different "voices" in telling the story and thereby avoid the risk of his narrative being too one-dimensional. The viewpoint (the events being told in hindsight, reconstructed from different sources) also allows Fitzgerald to build and maintain suspense – who *is* Gatsby? Where does his money come from? – as his narrator presents his story in a mosaic-like manner, not always chronological, and not always from the same perspective.
There are patterns of imagery throughout the novel, most importantly the weather, seasons and colours, which provide a constantly-shifting reflection of and commentary on the characters and events.

Seasons and the weather

Here are some examples of how Fitzgerald makes use of the weather to comment on or reflect the mood of the characters or the pressure of events.

TEXT	REFERENCE	ANALYSIS
I came east, permanently, I thought, in the spring of twenty-two. [...] And so with the sunshine and the great bursts of leaves growing on the trees [...] I had that familiar conviction that life was beginning over again with the summer.	p. 9 l. 3–p. 10 l. 4	The story told by Nick begins in Spring, when life begins after the sleep of winter: the story grows out of spring and ends in autumn when natural things begin to die or withdraw to the safety of hibernation. This framing of the corrupt, human events of the story within the order of nature's cyclical structure can be read as an ironic comment on humanity's inability to escape nature, no matter how advanced we become; it also implies hope and freshness and new life, and provides a subtly vast context for the story. The careful use of mythical and magical symbols and references in the novel makes the symbolism of the seasons even more potent.
The late afternoon sky bloomed in the window for a moment like the blue honey of the Mediterranean – then the shrill voice of Mrs. McKee called me back into the room.	p. 50 l. 26–p. 51 l. 3	Nick would like to leave the stuffy, drunken party at Myrtle's apartment. The world outside represents natural calm and beauty (blooming like a flower, sweet like honey, clear and clean like the blue waters of the Mediterranean) – and above all escape.

TEXT	REFERENCE	ANALYSIS
The day agreed upon was pouring rain. "One of the papers said they thought the rain would stop about four." The rain cooled about half past three to a damp mist. Once more it was pouring […] After half an hour the sun shone again […] While the rain had continued it had seemed like the murmur of their voices, rising and swelling a little, now and then, with gusts of emotion. But in the new silence I felt that silence had fallen within the house too. "It's stopped raining." "Has it?" When he realized what I was talking about, that there were twinkle-bells of sunshine in the room, he smiled like a weather man, like an ecstatic patron of recurrent light […] Outside the wind was loud and there was a faint flow of thunder along the Sound.	Chapter V (pp. 111–131)	Chapter V, in which Gatsby and Daisy are reunited, is filled with weather imagery and symbolism. The day begins with heavy rain: Gatsby's belief that it will stop at about four comes true. It does: when Daisy arrives. Rain suggests tears and Daisy has been crying when Nick returns. Rain is also cleansing. It makes things seem fresh and new. Gatsby's association with the sun in this scene is a specific example of how he is associated with summer, and therefore with the sun: with its power to warm (his love) and nurture (his generosity) with its heat and light (his wealth). This is the story of Gatsby and the summer. As far as we the readers are concerned, in Nick's narrative Gatsby only exists, like a butterfly, for one summer. He has a mysterious, distant past, and when the summer is finished (with Myrtle's death) he must die. The rising wind and distant thunder are omens, far away for now and easy to ignore, of the tragedy that this meeting will cause. The thunder is an ominous rumbling coming from the direction of New York city.

TEXT	REFERENCE	ANALYSIS
The next day was broiling, almost the last, certainly the warmest, of the summer. In this heat every extra gesture was an affront to the common store of life. "I read somewhere that the sun's getting hotter every year," said Tom genially. "It seems that pretty soon the earth's going to fall into the sun – or wait a minute – it's just the opposite – the sun's getting colder every year." Gatsby's eyes floated toward her. "Ah," she cried, "you look so cool." "You always look so cool," she repeated. The relentless heat was beginning to confuse me and I had a bad moment there before I realized that so far his suspicions hadn't alighted on Tom. "I love New York on summer afternoons when everyone's away. There's something very sensuous about it – overripe..."	Chapter VII (pp.151–191)	This critical episode in the story is accompanied by an oppressive and uncomfortable heat from which there is no escape. As Nick returns from the city the heat becomes unbearable. Everything is exhausted, stagnant and damp with sweat. People are irritable and uncomfortable. Daisy telling Gatsby how cool he looks is the first move in the disaster that now slowly unfolds. Like alcohol (see Chapter II), heat can distort perception and alter consciousness. Nick has trouble concentrating on – and recalling – what happens. The heat represents the climax of the summer – of the story – and the mounting pressure which comes to a crisis in the encounter between Gatsby and Tom. Tom "wins" and the summer, which has been closely associated with Gatsby, is over. By the time Daisy and Gatsby leave, the heat has passed. The pressure has broken and the dreams of summer have died: Daisy stays with Tom, Myrtle is dead, Nick has seen clearly how shallow these people all are.

TEXT	REFERENCE	ANALYSIS
"The thing to do is forget about the heat," said Tom impatiently. "You make it ten times worse by crabbing about it." So we drove on toward death through the cooling twilight.		
The night had made a sharp difference in the weather and there was an autumn flavor in the air.	p. 199. ll. 14–17	Myrtle's death literally marks the end of the summer. Now things grow colder. The warmth and life of the summer climaxed in oppressive heath, followed by death. Gatsby and Myrtle, the doomed dreamers, die and Daisy, the fairy-tale princess, returns to her cruel husband.
About five o'clock our procession of three cars reached the cemetery and stopped in a thick drizzle beside the gate [...] I tried to think about Gatsby then for a moment but he was already too far away [...]	p. 225 l. 3–p. 226 l. 5	Gatsby's funeral is a lonely event with few people attending. The rain here is sad and autumnal. Nick is saying goodbye to Gatsby in a setting and in weather in which all traces of the man have vanished along with the summer.

Ambiguity

Fitzgerald uses ambiguity to subvert the characters and events. Nothing is clear-cut and wholly admirable: nothing is pure. This is occasionally ironic or satirical, as when Tom's hypocrisy is made apparent in his rants about traditional family values.

THE AMBIGUITY	
"Great" Gatsby	While Gatsby is corrupt, his dream is incorruptible (see p. 200 ll. 24–28). Gatsby is presented from the beginning (p. 6 l. 18–p. 7 l. 15) until the end (p. 200 ll. 14–28) as someone who is apparently deserving of contempt, a criminal and a materialistic, flamboyant example of „New Money". But Nick finds it impossible to condemn him. Gatsby's charm and the purity of his motivations are in constant conflict with the world around him.
Jordan	Both blunt and dishonest (see pp. 82–83), Jordan is ambiguous for both Nick and the reader. He is terribly disappointed by her shallowness and selfishness, yet he feels "half in love with her, and tremendously sorry" (p. 230 ll. 1–2) when he finally breaks with her.
Daisy	While Daisy epitomises the desirable in the novel, she turns out to be shallow and selfish and more concerned with maintaining her status and security than with pursuing dreams of happiness with Gatsby. Nick comes to understand that she lives in an "artificial world" (p. 196 l. 12) and that there is little substance behind her mask of beauty. Early on Nick is struck by the divide between her polished exterior and the hidden currents underneath (p. 29 ll. 9–24).
Tom	"I was tempted to laugh whenever he opened his mouth. The transition from libertine to prig was so complete" (p. 172 l. 28–p. 173 l. 2). The base instincts and arrogance of the highest-born character in the story, Tom, overwhelm everything he might stand for. An adulterous hypocrite who rants about the erosion of family values, his brutality and snobbery make him a caricature of the privileged rich.

THE AMBIGUITY	
Cars	Cars are carefully and consistently associated throughout the novel with both desire and death. As with other features of the modern age they are treated ambiguously by Fitzgerald as things which enable greater freedom and irresponsibility, individualism and selfishness, fun and carelessness and are intrinsically dangerous.
The past	The origins of the characters and their dreams are seldom clear and never unambiguous. Nick enjoys the wildness of the East until the end of the summer when he longs to return to his childhood home. Gatsby's past is both a source of inescapable shame and the fuel for his dreams. For Daisy, the past is done with. She had forgotten Gatsby until she heard Jordan mention him.

Colours

White: purity and innocence

Colours are carefully associated throughout the novel with Daisy (white) and Gatsby (yellow). These colours traditionally symbolise purity and innocence (white) and happiness and sunshine (yellow). Their use here shifts from the serious to the ironic and these shifting emphases influence the reader's understanding of the characters. They are also suggestions ("gold-hatted" / "silver idols") which associate them with gold (Gatsby) and silver (Daisy), and thus with the sun and the moon, strongly charged mythical symbols of male and female power. Importantly, Tom's racist theories give the colour of purity and innocence a sharply satirical corrective.

CHARACTER	COLOUR	REFERENCE
Daisy	White	...the white palaces of fashionable East Egg...p. 12.l. 19 [Daisy and Jordan] were both in white... p. 17 l. 2 "Our white girlhood was passed together there." (p. 31 ll. 27–28) She was [...] by far the most popular of all the girls in Louisville. She dressed in white and had a little white roadster... (p. 104 ll. 6–9) It wasn't until then that I connected this Gatsby with the officer in her white car. (p. 108 l. 21–22) His heart beat faster and faster as Daisy's white face came up to his own. (p. 150 ll. 7–8) Daisy and Jordan lay upon an enormous couch, like silver idols, weighing down their own white dresses... (p. 154 ll. 16–17) High in a white palace the king's daughter... (p. 160 l. 25) Daisy, glowing like silver... (p. 195 l. 6) He stayed there for a week [...] revisiting the out-of-the-way places to which they had driven in her white car. (p. 198 ll. 15–18)
Gatsby	Yellow	The novel's epigraph about the "gold-hatted, high-bouncing lover" associates Gatsby's wealth with a showy display intended solely to catch Daisy's attention. It both mocks the intention ("if you can bounce high, bounce for her too") and condemns the shallowness of Daisy's reaction. Gatsby's yellow car is associated with joy and excitement ("brisk yellow bug" p. 56 l. 16) and Nick thinks it is gorgeous (see pp. 88–89), but it comes to be known as the "death car" (p. 181 l. 14) and its bright colour makes it easier to identify. There is a brief, haunting foreshadowing of his yellow car when he tells Nick the story of his time with Daisy years ago (p. 198 l.23–p. 199 l.3).

CHARACTER	COLOUR	REFERENCE
		Gatsby's association with yellow (joy and optimism) is ironically undercut, as is Daisy's with white. Whereas her purity is revealed as selfishness, his identification with sunlight and happiness leads to his own death and the end of summer.
Tom	White	"The idea is if we don't look out the white race will be – will be utterly submerged." pp. 23–24 "... intermarriage between black and white" p. 172
Various	Blue	The colour blue is associated with escape. Tom's car, which George wants so badly, is blue. When Nick wishes to escape from Myrtle's party he longs for the "blue honey" of outside (p. 51 l. 1). The magical world Gatsby creates is referred to as his "blue gardens" (p. 56 l. 6) and "blue lawn" (p. 233 l. 15). In the oppressive heat of Chapter VII the distant, cool sea is described as the "blue, cool limit" (p. 158 ll. 1–2).
Daisy and Gatsby	Green	The green light on Daisy's dock (first mentioned p. 34 ll. 16–20) is one of the major symbols in the novel. It represents Daisy's desirability for Gatsby and his unattainable dream. It only has relevance for him, and once he has "achieved" it loses its meaning (p. 127 ll. 9–20). For Nick however it has great significance: it is the final image he gives us (p. 233 ll. 21–27).
George Wilson	Grey	George is stranded in the valley of ashes (see pp. 34–36). The colour represents lifeless, depressed despair. He has been emasculated by Tom, who steals his wife, and he stands for the "losers" of the modern age – as opposed to "winners" like Tom and Gatsby. George is tied to a dead waste land, drained of life and hope.

Narrative tone

The language used throughout the novel is all Nick's, as narrator: but he makes use of different sources and these give the novel a diversified texture and tone.

PASSAGE	REFERENCE	TONE
Gatsby remembers kissing Daisy	pp. 149–150	This text has the transcendent, unreal quality of someone blinded by love. Nick himself describes Gatsby's words as "appalling sentimentality".
Gatsby recalls falling in love with Daisy	pp. 192–7	This longer passage is reported by Nick and told directly by Gatsby and serves to give a clearer picture of the story Jordan had only observed in fragments (pp. 103–108). The passage is honest in a way that little of Gatsby's stories have been before now. He is open about his own dishonesty and poor background. The combination of Gatsby's own words and Nick's interpretation further enhances the credibility of what is being narrated here.
Daisy's conversation	pp. 17–32	When Daisy talks it is clear that her ironic, witty conversation is designed for effect. She wants to entertain and enchant. In contrast to Tom's clumsy directness and confused theories, Daisy uses all her charms to create the impression of having done "gay, exciting things just a while since and that there were gay, exciting things hovering in the next hour" (p. 18 ll. 22–23).

PASSAGE	REFERENCE	TONE
Jordan describes Daisy's youth and first meeting with Gatsby	pp.103–108	Jordan's narrative tone, as passed on by Nick, is cooler than his own. She has a laconic descriptive style which sets the scene and, like Nick, can portray people without judging them.
Nick reconstructs the events of the night of Myrtle's death, using accounts from Michaelis and the police	pp. 180–181 pp. 208–209	The precision and distanced tone of these passages not only provides yet more variety in the texture of the book, it also effectively juxtaposes an objective coolness with the terrible events being described: Myrtle's death, George's grief, and the events leading to Gatsby's murder.
Nick describes Gatsby's appearance	p. 69. ll. 15–30	In this passage Nick analyses in detail Gatsby's smile, the outward symbol of his great charm.
Nick looks back as he leaves	p. 233	At the close of the novel Nick is struggling to find a way to express the complex insights he has been granted. Whereas he began to narrate the novel by giving a clear and uncomplicated portrait of himself and his background, he ends with a symbolic interpretation of the meaning of the green light.

3.7 Interpretation

The Great Gatsby has gone through ups and downs in popularity since publication. There have been two major Hollywood adaptations (in 1974 and 2013) as well as other film versions, and it has had widespread influence in other media. It combines a story which continues to move, excite or fascinate readers with its complex and layered portrait of both a specific era in American society and the development of American myths and ideals. Approaches to the novel have focussed on different aspects. Three major areas of interest are:

→ gender – the presentation and interaction of men and women in the novel, which is rich with irony and mythical connotations;
→ the idea and ideals of American identity and the myths of The Frontier;
→ the modern world of mass culture and consumerism, and the effects it has on society and on individuals.

Reactions to each of these topics are influenced by the society and era from which they are being viewed.

Fitzgerald's use of themes in other works

These themes – gender, the ideals of American identity and the modern world of mass culture and consumerism – are among the most prevalent in Fitzgerald's major works, and it can be very useful when studying *Gatsby* to also read the story collection *All the Sad Young Men* for a similarly sad and doubting examination of the modern world. The novel *Tender is the Night* is an excellent look at aspects of the modern age and lifestyles and their effect on personal relationships. Fitzgerald was a writer who remained true to specific themes which interested him and with which he was familiar, and the social and moral issues raised by the changing world of the 1920s dominated his writing up until the end.

Gender

Gender roles and interactions are of considerable interest in *The Great Gatsby*. Daisy is identified with a Siren (a mythological creature who uses her seductive charms to lure men to their doom) and Myrtle is presented as a more physical, sensual woman with a stronger sexual appetite. The male characters in the novel struggle for possession of the women (Daisy and Myrtle), with the exception of Nick, whose relationship to women is very different from Tom's dominant, aggressive attitude and Gatsby's transcendent desire.

Daisy is "excitingly desirable" and is at the centre of the novel's conflict, as her husband and lover struggle to possess her. She is very good at making herself interesting to men:

> "I've heard it said that Daisy's murmur was only to make people lean toward her: an irrelevant criticism that makes it no less charming." (p. 18 ll. 3–6)

And, Jordan suggests, at concealing her own indiscretions:

> "They moved with a fast crowd, but she came out with an absolutely perfect reputation. Perhaps because she doesn't drink. It's a great advantage not to drink among hard drinking people. You can hold your tongue and, moreover, you can time any little irregularity of your own so that everybody else is so blind that they don't see or care. Perhaps Daisy never went in for amour at all – and yet there's something in that voice of hers..." (p. 108 ll. 5–13)

Exposing Daisy layer by layer

Fitzgerald is careful to establish Daisy's seductive beauty and air of thrilling mystery before peeling back the layers. She has forgotten Gatsby and, no matter how exciting she finds him, how much she loves to be loved and adored, what she most desires is the security and status which only Tom can give her. The secret world the two of them share is impenetrable to outsiders – neither Nick, Gatsby nor the reader can penetrate to what it is that holds the two of them together, unless it really is love ("Even alone I can't say I never loved Tom," p. 176 l. 12) or their shared upper class world (Nick says that they "drifted here and there unrestfully wherever people played polo and were rich together", p. 13 ll. 18–19).

So while she is presented as a modern feminine ideal of exciting, charming beauty, the character of Daisy Buchanan is also exposed layer by layer to be much more manipulative and self-interested than she first appears.

Tom is almost a caricature of a brutish, "hulking" male figure. Nick has no illusions about him:

> "As for Tom the fact that he "had some woman in New York" was really less surprising than that he had been depressed by a book." (p. 33 ll. 6–8)

When he realises that Daisy loves Gatsby and that George wants to take Myrtle away, he feels the "hot whips of panic":

> "His wife and mistress, until an hour ago secure and inviolate, were slipping precariously from his control." (p. 166 ll .10–12)

Arrogance and possessiveness

His possessiveness and terror of losing "his" women to other men are further examples of his stereotypical "hulking brute" nature. His arrogance in his dealings with George are doubly vicious, as he is dominating George not only financially and socially, being so much wealthier and more privileged, but also sexually, as he has "taken" George's wife. Whereas Nick's relationships with women are more refined and Gatsby's love for Daisy is unreal in its devotion, Tom's is presented as being more immediately sexual. Myrtle tells Nick how they met (p. 53 ll. 6–19): his powerful physical presence excited her and she submitted to his dominant nature. Soon afterwards we see him hitting her for saying Daisy's name.

While we will never know what exactly passed between the two of them on the day after Myrtle's death, when Tom pointed George in the direction of Gatsby, the results were clear: Tom manages to permanently remove the two men with whom he is in competition for Myrtle and Daisy.

Gatsby has idealised Daisy to the point where the real woman could no longer live up to his dream version. While their first encounters were clearly sexual ("He took what he could get, ravenously and unscrupulously" p. 193 ll.26–7), things take an unexpected turn:

> "He had intended, probably, to take what he could and go – but now he found that he had committed himself to the following of a grail." (p. 194 ll. 14–16)

Purity and idealism

Gatsby is, paradoxically, a pure and almost asexual being, remarkable for his isolation and solitude: at his parties he is anonymous, standing alone, uninvolved and abstinent, while the crowds drink and dance and flirt around him. He is **fixated on an ideal from the past** and wants to recreate the past in an impossible, romantic act of reversal.

> "He wanted nothing less of Daisy than that she should go to Tom and say 'I never loved you.' After she had obliterated three years with that sentence they could decide upon the more practical measures to be taken. One of them was that, after she was free, they were to go back to Louisville and be married from her house – just as if it were five years ago." (p. 148 ll. 19–25)

The grail reference associates him with the mythical purity of the questing knights: only the purest knight can find the Holy Grail. But Gatsby is corrupted, by his lies, his secret past and his criminal enterprises. His purity is in his "incorruptible dreams" – while he himself is thoroughly corrupted. His isolation is complete, as he dies without love of any kind (except the friendship of Nick). He has lost part of himself in loving Daisy, almost as if a part of him has died, further establishing her identification with a seductive creature who destroys men.

Nick is the great exception to the rule. He is not driven by powerful passions and unreal expectations. He has brief relationships with women:

> "I even had a short affair with a girl who lived in Jersey City and worked in the accounting department but her brother began throwing mean looks in my direction so when she went on her vacation in July I let it blow quietly away." (p. 80 ll. 5–9)

But what characterises his attitude to women is his respect and decency. There are two examples of this in the novel:

> "...for a moment I thought I loved her. But I am slow thinking and full of interior rules that act as brakes on my desires, and I knew that first I had to get myself definitely out of that tangle

> back home. I'd been writing letters once a week and signing them "Love, Nick," and all I could think of was how, when that certain girl played tennis, a faint mustache of perspiration appeared on her upper lip. Nevertheless there was a vague understanding that had to be tactfully broken off before I was free." (p. 84 ll. 3–12)

> "There was one thing to be done before I left, an awkward, unpleasant thing that perhaps had better have been let alone. But I wanted to leave things in order and not just trust that obliging and indifferent sea to sweep my refuse away. I saw Jordan Baker and talked over and around what had happened to us together and what had happened afterward to me, and she lay perfectly still listening in a big chair." (p. 228 ll. 15-22)

Most positive male figure

In both instances Nick is driven by his better instincts to be honest and open to the women with whom he is involved, even if in both cases the relationship is largely finished. He likes to establish clarity and ensure that there is a minimum of messy, hurt feelings in his affairs. This decency is an obvious contrast to Tom's brutish possessiveness and Gatsby's unreal devotion, and as such Nick is shown to be the most positive male figure in the novel.

America/The Frontier

The myths of American identity have a lot to do with the idea of The Frontier and the freedom it represented to the pioneers who set out from the original European settlements in the East to explore the West. The sense that the pioneers were chasing a constantly receding frontier, and the dream of freedom for which it stood, is relevant to *The Great Gatsby*.

Changing American identities

The period in which the novel was written and is set was a **time of rapid change in society**. This led, in the arts as well as in politics and society, to a re-examination of American values and what it meant to be American. This uncertainty was a characteristic of American literature's Lost Generation. The sense of innocence lost, and the consequent quest to reclaim the dreams of youth – Gatsby's love for Daisy, Nick's memories of his childhood in the Midwest – can be read as Fitzgerald's treatment of America's disorientation in the face of a suddenly-modern world. The characters represent different faces of the American identity:

→ Gatsby the self-made man bridges the worlds of high society and the underworld, and embodies the contradictions of America's ideal of freedom and capitalist endeavour.
→ Tom comes from the powerful elite of old wealthy families: money allows him to move freely in an increasingly consumerist, capitalist society.
→ Daisy combines both a classic fairy-tale princess appeal with a very modern ideal of feminine attractiveness: as a beautiful woman from the upper class she embodies the ideal of American desirability.
→ George stands for the losers of the modern world: encouraged by progress but held back by those with more money and power.
→ Myrtle, like George, is the face of a poor working class which aspires in vain to the fashions, freedom and lifestyle of the wealthier classes.
→ Jordan is the ideal of the modern young woman, independent, cynical and cool.
→ Nick is a hybrid of traditional Midwest society and a new, introspective and cautious generation trying to find their place in a changed world.

→ Dan Cody, Gatsby's "second father" and great inspiration, is an adventurer, a relic of a lost age (see pp. 135–137): he makes his fortune in the "savage violence" of the frontier, and is ruined by his own success.

Nick points out that they all came from the West, highlighting the deep-rooted contradictions within American identity:

> "I see now that this has been a story of the West after all – Tom and Gatsby, Daisy and Jordan and I, were all Westerners, and perhaps we possessed some deficiency in common which made us subtly unadaptable to Eastern life." (p. 227 ll. 12–16)

A major theme in American literature is **the tension between the Old World (Europe) and the New (the USA)**. It was a dominant theme in the work of Henry James, in whose work the tension was usually located in the corrupting influence of the Old World on the innocence of the New (what James called 'the international theme'). Here in *Gatsby* we have something similar at work, but with the corrupting influence of the old world being recast to the modern corruption of the East coast, specifically New York.

The corrupting East

Nick feels corrupted by his contact with the East (see his distorted nightmare vision on pp. 227–228), and by the end he longs for the comfort and familiarity of his home state, remembering childhood journeys by train. He wants to return to an ideal which – no less than Gatsby's idealisation of Daisy – is an illusion, a memory. His idealised American "heartland" is a composite of traditional values and ideals which, as with all ideals, can never be real. At the end of the novel he considers the Dutch sailors who settled Manhattan and how they encountered – for the last time in history – a space which would be big enough to contain their dreams and desires.

This idea of the potential of the American continent to provide a frontier in which freedom can be pursued is touched with the same sad sense of loss as is Gatsby's love for Daisy: like the frontier withdrawing as the pioneers progressed, the dreams of the characters recede as they advance.

The modern world

There were great changes in lifestyle and society during the period in which The Great Gatsby is set and was written, and these can be seen in the novel. Both Nick and Gatsby had served in the First World War: Gatsby "did extraordinarily well in the war" (p. 195 l. 29), he was rapidly promoted and presented with medals for bravery. After the war, back in America, the uniform gives him a certain protection from social discrimination, but by the time Meyer Wolfshiem discovers him he is starving and penniless (see p. 220–221). Nick enjoyed his service so much (p. 8 ll. 9–15) that he felt restless when he returned to the US that, instead of "being the warm center of the world the middle-west now seemed like the ragged edge of the universe". The war was a reversal of the westwards-driven frontier myth: young American men now went back to the Old World in their thousands.

Service in WWI

Both men are changed by their time in the army and their experience of WWI. While Nick is invigorated by it and finds that it has both broadened his horizons and filled him with restless discontent, for Gatsby it was a time in which he tried to lose himself ("I tried very hard to die but I seemed to bear an enchanted life" p. 91 ll. 16–17) and from which he emerged with nothing but a uniform and a very brief period spent studying at Oxford University in England. It was only the uniform which had made it possible for Daisy and he to meet in the first place, before the war – Daisy had lived near Camp Taylor where Gatsby was stationed, and she was popular with the young officers (see p. 104). After the war he has nothing left. Daisy has left him to marry Tom and he is broke and unemployed. Wolfshiem sees his ambition and energy – and the veneer of class he has acquired from his brief stay in Oxford – and realises he can use him (see p. 221).

Tom during the war

We learn nothing about what Tom did during the war. It is implied that he didn't serve, because obviously he was there to court and then marry Daisy while Nick and Gatsby were in Europe. **Tom's wealth and status and life are not altered or interrupted or energised by the war**, as was the case with Nick and Gatsby. His wealthy lifestyle continues regardless. Tom and Daisy belong to a powerful upper class whose fortunes are stable and unshakable. They move on into the post-war modern world with ease, secure in a closed society of the rich and playful.

The Wilsons serve as a counterpoint to this. It is unclear whether George served during the war, although it seems unlikely: no mention is made of it. Both George and Myrtle are trapped in the hopeless life of the working class. While Myrtle tries to imitate what she thinks is the lifestyle of a woman Tom would be involved with, George is denied any kind of escape, even one as false as Myrtle's.

The powerlessness of the Wilsons

Myrtle tries to break out and assume what she thinks are the attitudes and behaviour of the elite she so envies – at the party in Chapter III she constantly changes her clothes as if uncertain of how she should look and what sort of impression she should be trying to make, and her attitude becomes increasingly bossy and dominant as if to compensate for her powerlessness in her real life. George is trapped in the valley of ashes with no escape. The giant eyes of the billboard which watch over him constantly, and which he later associates with the eyes of God, suggest that in this modern world, **symbols of consumerism and materialism** (advertisements) have replaced spiritual or moral orientation. He longs for Tom's car, for the escape it seems to promise him. He is closely linked to the idea of the car as status symbol – in his case an unreachable one – and his life among the ashes identifies him as society's unwanted refuse: lacking Tom's privileges or Gatsby's desire and ambition, **George is the great loser of the modern world**, unable to participate in the pleasures and freedoms of the consumerist, hedonist age.

Disorientation of modern life

The Wilsons live where they work, which is an important distinction and a sign of the times: Nick can afford to commute to his workplace from the suburbs of Long Island, a modern convenience. Gatsby's work – national in scale – seems to be largely conducted via the telephone, another very modern convenience. Jordan is a professional golfer, an extremely fashionable and very modern life for a young woman in the 1920s, when the sport had only recently been liberated from being an exclusively male, upper class pastime. And neither Tom nor Daisy need to work.

The world Fitzgerald has created underlines the **shallowness and disorientation of modern life** in an age in which spiritual and moral certainties have vanished or been distorted. But it also points to the fundamental injustice of traditional American societal structures, in which, in spite of the democratic ideals of the country, wealth and class dominate social interaction. By the end of the novel society's "losers" – the Wilsons – are both dead, as is Gatsby, "Mr Nobody from Nowhere" (p. 172 ll. 16–17). Those characters who came from the upper classes, wealthy and stable, continue with their lives: Tom and Daisy have moved on again, leaving behind the mess they created, and Nick has returned to the home of which he had become bored after the First World War. The East, representing the lively, exciting modern age, is seen at the end of the novel as corrupt and deformed.

4. CRITICAL RECEPTION

The Great Gatsby was considered Fitzgerald's greatest achievement as a writer, but when he died the general consensus was that while he had shown great promise (with *Gatsby*), he had been unable to develop on this early triumph. In spite of praise from other writers, his reputation remained low until, beginning in the 1960s with the mass market distribution of *Gatsby* in a paperback format, he was reintroduced to a broader audience and as a result re-evaluated in several biographies and critical studies. *The Great Gatsby* in particular continues to attract attention, both as a work of American literature which is accessible to repeated and diverse analyses, and as an immensely popular story (with another major Hollywood film adaptation in 2013) which still fascinates and entertains.

Contemporary reviewers were delighted with *The Great Gatsby*, appreciating **Fitzgerald's humour and eye for human details** and the great care he took with the form and structure of the novel. He had been a familiar figure on the literary scene for some time already, and was firmly associated with the Jazz Age – he was referred to as "the philosopher of the flapper". *Gatsby* proved that he could mature as a writer. He was known for being a witty and astute observer of the young generation, but *Gatsby* took a more mature view of a slightly older group of characters.

Respect as a serious writer

The effort he made to tell a story about "his" crowd – the flappers, the Lost Generation – growing up was respected by critics, as was the more innovative structure of the novel. He had always

TV-production *The Great Gatsby* with Mira Sorvino and Toby Stephens (UK/USA 2000). © Cinetext/ Sammlung Richter

been recognised as a good writer, someone who could write prettily, sadly or wittily, but *Gatsby* owed more to the early Modernist narrative techniques of Joseph Conrad – especially the narration of *Heart of Darkness* – than did his earlier stories. This won him more respect as a serious writer. He received letters from other writers, including Edith Wharton (like Henry James before her and Fitzgerald himself, a great chronicler of East Coast life and society) and T.S. Eliot (who considered that the book signalled the first great development in American literature since Henry James). But despite this respect and acclaim **the book was a commercial disappointment** and his reputation as the flapper philosopher coloured many responses.

In an obituary in the *New York Times* from December 23, 1940, his career is summarised as having roughly begun and ended with the 1920s: the "best of his books" is said to be *The Great Gatsby*, and otherwise the "promise of his brilliant career was never fulfilled". His other novels were largely dismissed, apart from *This Side of Paradise*, which kept a certain distinction as being the novel which, as Gertrude Stein said, created "the new generation" in the public imagination.

1930–1940

In the years following its publication the novel was viewed mostly as a piece of light fiction, a delightful but nostalgic work about a very specific and very brief era in American history. This was a **major disappointment for Fitzgerald**, who had been aware while writing the novel that it was his most ambitious attempt and also greatest achievement. The critic Matthew Josephson wrote in an article in 1933 that Fitzgerald should remember that there were Americans "who can't drink champagne from morning to night". A year later another critic wrote of the book that it treated sensuality – an important factor in such a highly-charged love story – as being "half flippant and half sentimental". In the same year, 1934, the book was included in the Library of America, but was dropped in 1939.

Throughout the 1930s and into the 1940s mainstream discussion of Fitzgerald and his writing was rather condescending, focussing on his well-publicised private life, from the mental illness of his wife Zelda to his own struggle with alcoholism. Fitzgerald's publisher Scribner's loyally kept the book in print through the years, despite its sinking reputation, and it maintained a small but steady readership which, by the time of his death in 1940, had come to include future writers who were influenced by its evocative, atmospheric story and writing as well as by its finely-structured form. By 1945 critical opinion had moved from dismissing *The Great Gatsby* as a period piece, light nostalgia from a professional entertainer, to a more serious appreciation of the novel for itself, not just as an aspect of the author's celebrated, tragically short life.

Themes of American lives

In the 1940s critics began to reassess the figure of Jay Gatsby as "one of the few truly mythological creations in our culture" and to pay attention to Fitzgerald's examination of themes of American lives. Of equal importance was an increasing recognition of the "voice" of the novel – meaning not only the powerfully evocative language, but also the "voice" of **Nick Carraway** as a complex and sympathetic **ideal of American identity**, educated, ironic, morally sound and compassionate.

By the 1960s there was still a variety of opinions about Fitzgerald's value as a writer but there was little dissent over the status of *The Great Gatsby* as **an American classic**. Several studies were published on his work and the book became required reading in schools and universities. The major scholar of Fitzgerald's writing is Matthew J. Bruccoli (1931–2008), whose books have become the standard reference for all contemporary research into Fitzgerald's life and works. Studies of *The Great Gatsby* in recent years have concentrated largely on **issues of class and gender**. There have also been discussions of the presentation of racism in the book, and the changing concerns and interests of society continue to open new perspectives on the themes of desire, inequality, ambition, wealth, social status and the nature of the American dream.

5. MATERIALS

Contemporary reactions

"An author ought to write for the youth of his own generation, the critics of the next, and the school masters of ever afterward." Fitzgerald's own words are prophetic. *The Great Gatsby* received positive reviews, but was also treated condescendingly and dismissively. It sold reasonably, but not well enough to satisfy the author or silence his critics. Critical recognition was slow in coming: by the time he died Fitzgerald had largely been forgotten and it was not until the 1960s that the book acquired the status it now has – of a classic of American literature. Almost 80 years later it is required reading around the world.

The *New York Times* review in 1925 continued to identify Fitzgerald as the chronicler of the Jazz Age generation.

"Of the many new writers that sprang into notice with the advent of the post-war period, Scott Fitzgerald has remained the steadiest performer and the most entertaining. Short stories, novels and a play have followed with consistent regularity since he became the philosopher of the flapper with *This Side of Paradise*. With shrewd observation and humor he reflected the Jazz Age. Now he has said farewell to his flappers – perhaps because they have grown up – and is writing of the older sisters that have married. But marriage has not changed their world, only the locale of their parties. [...] his hurt romantics are still seeking that other side of paradise. And it might almost be said that *The Great Gatsby* is the last stage of illusion in this absurd chase. For middle age is certainly creeping up on Mr. Fitzgerald's flappers."

Fitzgerald had written "a conflict of spirituality set against the web of our commercial life", a book of "whimsical magic and simple pathos that is realized with economy and restraint". The reviewer compares the narrative structure to Henry James' *The Turn of the Screw*, commenting that the two works are more long short stories than novels.

Fitzgerald's goal had been to "write something *new*–something extraordinary and beautiful and simple + intricately patterned". Fellow writers understood that he had indeed accomplished this – Gertrude Stein praised it and T.S. Eliot called it "the first step American fiction has taken since Henry James".

Re-assessment

Critic Lionel Trilling

Critic Lionel Trilling suggested in 1945 that Gatsby could be interpreted as symbolising America itself. This approach provided something of a breakthrough in establishing the novel's reputation as more than a pretty, melodramatic love story of the Jazz Age. Almost 60 years later, American author Jay McInerney (*Bright Lights, Big City*) confirms the validity of this approach: "Fitzgerald's prose somehow elevates a lurid and underdeveloped narrative to the level of myth." McInerney sees the novel as the key to American identity: "It's more than an American classic; it's become a defining document of the national psyche, a creation myth." With the benefit of distance it is possible to appreciate the novel's narrative structure: "Without Fitzgerald's poetry, without the editorial consciousness of Fitzgerald's narrator Nick Carraway, the story can seem threadbare and melodramatic." With greater distance from the era being described, and stripped of the nostalgia and overfamiliarity which would have affected critics nearer to the time, McInerney identifies the strengths of the book as being the quality of Fitzgerald's writing – which had never been called into question – and cites this as being the reason for the artistic failure of the film adaptations of the novel. Without Nick's voice as narrator and Fitzgerald's evocative prose, what is left is a mythological love story about the American Dream: "Fitzgerald's *Gatsby* is a very fragile creation, made of words and dreams."

Fitzgerald looks back on the Jazz Age

One of the obstacles the novel, and Fitzgerald as a writer, had to overcome was the inextricable connection to the over-hyped Jazz Age. A period in society which was marked by such an obsessive self-awareness, thanks to the innovations of new media, and which ended so abruptly with an economic depression, was doomed to be either glorified or treated with embarrassed contempt by its own generation and that which followed. Fitzgerald himself, having given the period its name and been its most prominent and celebrated spokesman, eulogized the Jazz Age in his 1931 essay *Echoes of the Jazz Age*.

"It ended two years ago, because the utter confidence which was its essential prop received an enormous jolt, and it didn't take long for the flimsy structure to settle earthward. And after two years the Jazz Age seems as far away as the days before the War. It was borrowed time anyhow — the whole upper tenth of a nation living with the insouciance of grand dukes and the casualness of chorus girls. But moralizing is easy now and it was pleasant to be in one's twenties in such a certain and unworried time. Even when you were broke you didn't worry about money, because it was in such profusion around you. Towards the end one had a struggle to pay one's share; it was almost a favour to accept hospitality that required any travelling. Charm, notoriety, mere good manners weighed more than money as a social asset. This was rather splendid, but things were getting thinner and thinner as the eternal necessary human values tried to spread over all that expansion. Writers were geniuses on the strength of one respectable book or play; just as during the War officers of four months' experience commanded hundreds of men, so there were now many little fish lording it over great big bowls. In the theatrical world extravagant productions were carried by a few second-rate stars, and so on up the scale into politics, where it was difficult to interest good men in positions of the highest importance and responsibility, importance and responsibility far exceeding that of business executives but which paid only five or six thousand a year.

Now once more the belt is tight and we summon the proper expression of horror as we look back at our wasted youth. Sometimes, though, there is a ghostly rumble among the drums, an asthmatic whisper in the trombones that swings me back into the early twenties when we drank wood alcohol and every day in every way grew better and better, and there was a first abortive shortening of the skirts, and girls all looked alike in sweater dresses, and people you didn't want to know said 'Yes, we have no bananas', and it seemed only a question of a few years before the older people would step aside and let the world be run by those who saw things as they were — and it all seems rosy and romantic to us who were young then, because we will never feel quite so intensely about our surroundings any more."[19]

The 1974 film

Robert Redford starred as Gatsby, Mia Farrow was Daisy and Bruce Dern played Tom in Jack Clayton's film, the screenplay for which was written by Francis Ford Coppola. The film was very popular

Robert Redford, Mia Farrow and Bruce Dern in *The Great Gatsby*

---

19 http://fitzgerald.narod.ru/crackup/056e-eho.htm

and successful, but has been criticised for its sentimentality (when Daisy is in the picture the camera is almost always in soft focus) and simplification of the narrative. While Coppola's screenplay is faithful to the book is cannot compensate for the loss of Nick's narrative voice. He is reduced to the role of a spectator and minor participant, removing his function as careful and moral observer and commentator, and what is left is a sad and lovely story of doomed love and tragic death. A contemporary reviewer wrote that the book "is a good deal more than an ill-fated love story about the cruelties of the idle rich," but that the film "can't see this through all its giant closeups of pretty knees and dancing feet. It's frivolous without being much fun".

6. SAMPLE EXAM QUESTIONS WITH ANSWERS

Unter www.königserläuterungen.de/download finden Sie im Internet zwei weitere Aufgaben mit Musterlösungen.

Die Zahl der Sternchen bezeichnet das Anforderungsniveau der jeweiligen Aufgabe.

Task 1*

Nick says: "There are only the pursued, the pursuing, the busy and the tired." (Chapter IV) How relevant is this idea to the characters in the novel?

Model answer:

FOUR CATEGORIES

Nick has this thought at the end of Chapter IV, which has taken the reader on a tour of the world of the novel: this panorama of impressions includes a glimpse of Wilson working in the valley of ashes (p.94 ll.26–9) and a list of the fashionable party crowd (pp.85–8), Nick's introduction to the criminal underworld (pp.96–103) and two different versions of Gatsby's history (pp.89–94 and 109–111). Nick has also quite explicitly compared the complicated emotional world of Gatsby and Daisy with the "clean, hard, limited" (p.110 l.28) Jordan Baker. This categorisation of people into four groups therefore comes straight after one of the most varied chapters in the novel, in terms of locations and characters, and can be seen as a kind of summary of what Nick and the reader have so far learned. Each of the characters in the novel fits in at least one of these categories.

Pursued

The word "pursued" can mean two things – depending on what is doing the chasing. Daisy is being pursued by Gatsby, whose love drives him to follow her. George Wilson is pursued by poverty and despair, Myrtle is pursued by frustration and the desire for a better life, Gatsby is pursued by his obsessive dreams, and Tom and Nick are both pursued by a vague restlessness. Many characters in the novel are chasing after things: some are pursuing a better life (George and Myrtle), or their dreams (Gatsby and the Wilsons). The crowds who attend Gatsby's parties are chasing fun and the pleasures of the moment. Wolfshiem, the gambler who manipulates betting on national sports events, is pursuing money. Nick is pursuing some kind of orientation after the First World War.

Tired – busy

The division of people into tired and busy also has different meanings. George Wilson is tired – physically and spiritually exhausted – of his hopeless life in the valley of ashes. Daisy is tired of Tom of his brutish arrogance, and Myrtle is tired of her husband. Nick and Jordan are busy people, alert and active: Nick is trying to establish a career for himself to fill the gap left by the excitement and energy he felt during his military service and Jordan is a professional sportswoman. The idea of being tired is not limited in the novel to physical weariness, but is extended to include the spiritual weariness and lack of direction and motivation which Fitzgerald felt affected his generation.

Task 2**

Discuss the geography of the novel – how do particular locations symbolise the social order?

Model answer:
The major locations used in the novel are West Egg, East Egg, the valley of ashes, and New York City. Each of these locations is specifically identified with characters or events: Gatsby lives in West Egg, Tom and Daisy live in East Egg, the Wilsons live in the valley of ashes, and the crisis of the plot – the confrontation between Tom and Gatsby over Daisy – occurs in the glamorous city.

East Egg – West Egg

The two Eggs are suburban towns on Long Island and East is more fashionable than West. This is also a further comment on the theme of divided American identities in the novel. The faster, more modern lifestyle and society of the East Coast are contrasted with the more traditional values and lifestyles of the Midwest, as when Nick compares the two on pages 227–8. On Long Island, East Egg is where the "white palaces" are (p.12 l.19), and is for Gatsby a distant symbol of desire, because he knows Daisy lives there: he watches it every night, looking at the green light on her dock. East Egg symbolises the substance, power and arrogance (Tom) and protected, seductive desirability (Daisy) of upper class society and lifestyles. West Egg on the other hand is "less fashionable" (p.11 l.20) but not poor. This is where new money and the wild urban classes come to party. Gatsby's mansion is, like his car, ridiculously flashy. Both are a source of delight, and reveal the gaudy taste of the newly wealthy. Gatsby's wealth but humbler origins are reflected in the geographical location of West Egg – so close yet still firmly separated by an expanse of water from the Eastern seat of power.

The valley of ashes

The valley of ashes symbolises the lower social orders, oppressed by the signs and symbols of modern progress and society – the billboards, the trains, the speeding cars, the waste and rubbish of the modern age in the huge ash heaps – and is home to George and Myrtle Wilson, who stand for the crushed and frustrated hopes and dreams of the lower classes in an accelerated world of commercialism and materialism. George spends his life working on other peoples' cars, tending symbolically to the dreams and freedoms of others, and Myrtle tries to escape from her unhappy life in mimicking what she thinks is the behaviour of ladies of a higher social order. Trapped between the suburbs, which the widespread availability of cars has made more convenient and desirable, and the city, the centre of commercial and fashionable activity, the valley of ashes symbolises the crushed and forgotten lower middle classes who are unable to benefit from the rapid changes of the modern world.

New York

New York represents the thriving capital of the Jazz Age, a place of tensions and excitement. It is a commercial centre (where Nick works, where Wolfshiem organises his business) and the place people go to have fun – even when the weather is so hot at the end of the summer Daisy suggests they go to New York. At the famous Plaza Hotel Tom and Gatsby confront each other. New York is associated with passion and tension and stormy behaviour, and this impression is made clear when Nick describes his nightmarish vision of the East (pp.227–8).

Task 3***

Analyse the literary techniques used by Fitzgerald to make Gatsby "great".

Model answer:

Ironical use of "great"

The adjective "great" is used ironically: what is great about Gatsby is at the same time undermined by his false identity and criminal activities. Because Nick is the narrator and says himself that Gatsby gave his name to the book (p.6 ll.16–17), we have to look at Nick's impression of Gatsby to understand what is meant by "great".

Gatsby is made to seem big and important because he is so mysterious. When Nick introduces him it is as someone who "represented everything for which I have an unaffected scorn" (p.6 l.18–p.7 l.1), but "Gatsby turned out all right in the end" (p.7 ll.11–12). The ambivalence of the character is established by the narrator from the beginning – and when we first "see" Gatsby it as a shadowy silhouette making a strange gesture in the dark towards a distant green light (p.34). Fitzgerald uses Nick as narrator to maintain this air of mystery. Nick is invited to one of the parties but Gatsby is nowhere to be seen. Guests at the party are spreading rumours about him, and the "romantic speculation" (p.64 l.7) adds an excitingly sinister element ("he killed a man once" p.63 ll.16–17) to the glamour.

Greatness of heart and strength

Fitzgerald uses the variety of voices available to his narrator to establish a series of incomplete glimpses of Gatsby before the man himself appears. And even when he does arrive, he remains elusive. His mannerisms ("old sport") are strange affectations, and his isolation sets him further apart (see p.79 l.16). The first explanation of his past that he gives Nick (p.90–3) is literally incredible (Nick says he feels while listening that he is "skimming hastily through a dozen magazines"), incomplete and inconsistent. He claims to be from the Midwest and then says San Francisco. Nick, as the narrator, is our eyes and ears in the novel, and Fitzgerald uses him to maintain a sense of uncertainty about Gatsby. As he learns more, hearing Jordan's story and later Gatsby's own, altered and expanded stories of his past, the mysteriously ambiguous character of Gatsby becomes more and more complete and yet remains ambivalent. It combines admirable qualities and terrible weaknesses. Nick's admiration makes him "great" in a genuine sense, for his greatness of heart and for the strength and purity of his dreams. But there is also a mocking tone to the "great" because he is a fake, someone who encourages "romantic speculation" about himself and leads people to believe that he studied at Oxford.

Symbol of America

Gatsby also becomes "great" through his symbolic identification with great ideas: as a symbol of America itself and as a symbol of the sun. Like America he escaped from oppressive beginnings, fell in love with an unreachable ideal, worked without scruples to create a self worthy of that ideal, only to find that he had been corrupted and that fantastic wealth has brought the dream no closer to reality. As a symbol of America's deep contradictions, its materialism and corruption as well as its boundless energy and visionary spirit, Gatsby is again "great" in both a genuinely respectful and mocking manner.

His identification with the sun links him to its warming, life-giving, joy-bringing powers, but also reminds the reader that the warmth and life of the sun only rules for the summer. Gatsby's story as told by Nick covers one summer. His era of greatness, his reign as the bright, wealthy, glamorous sun, ends with the summer and his death heralds the start of autumn (on the day of his murder "there was an autumn flavor in the air" p.199 ll.16). By symbolically associating Gatsby with two such huge concepts, Fitzgerald gives him an aura of greatness that makes his human frailty even sadder.

Task 4***

Defend *The Great Gatsby* against the accusation that it is merely a sentimental, nostalgic period piece.

Model answer:
Fitzgerald creates an aura of nostalgia (a feeling of sadness mixed with happiness when thinking of the past) and sentimentality (connected with emotions rather than with reason) in presenting the world he is describing. There are many things which seem to express a nostalgia for a certain lifestyle and freedom, in particular the descriptions of the parties at Gatsby's house in Chapters III and IV and the sense of rich young people rushing directionlessly around in search of fun and excitement. There is also a strong element of sentimentality – in the dramatic love story at the heart of the novel as well as in Gatsby's character and in his memories of the young Daisy. The scope of the novel, covering one summer, also contributes to the sense of nostalgia and sentimentality in showing how somthing carefree and beautiful can flourish for a brief moment and then wither and die with the changing seasons. The language used is intensely evocative, conjuring up sad and lovely images and often suggesting the ghostly memories which haunt the story.

The winners are the cold, hard and cool ones

There is however a consistent effort made to undercut the sentimentality, and the novel itself confronts the very idea of nostalgia. The bitter truth about Daisy's inadequacy as a suitable object for Gatsby's affections is that she is shallow and selfish. His immature idealisation and emotional fixation on Daisy is also irrational. Her pleasure in being courted by such a charming, adoring lover is also sentimental, irrational, ill-considered and insubstantial, collapsing immediately when it meets reality, as do Gatsby's dreams when confronted with Tom's "hard malice". The sentimentality in the novel is a fragile and hollow thing, too weak to survive in the world Fitzgerald is describing. There is nothing to either save or justify it: in a capitalist, consumerist world of materialism and selfish status-seeking, characters like Gatsby and George Wilson, both of whom are trying to escape from their pasts, are doomed. The "winners" are the cold, hard and cool ones, like Jordan, who moves swiftly on from being disappointed in Nick to getting engaged to a new man, and Tom, whose money and lack of sentimentality (sensitivity) protect him from the consequences of his and Daisy's actions.

Dangerous illusion

Nostalgia is a powerful theme in the novel and describes the motivation behind Gatsby's career and actions. Having been, as a young man, involved with the princess-like Daisy, he has become obsessed with his original memories of her. His energies are devoted to recreating that moment in time, to chasing dreams of a past life. Like Nick's vividly nostalgic memories of travelling home by train as a schoolboy (pp.226–7) these are memories of things which have gone. Rather than rewarding his characters' indulgence in nostalgia, Fitzgerald punishes them. Gatsby is killed for trying to turn back time and recapture the sadness and happiness of his time with Daisy. Daisy herself, while avoiding the responsibility for killing Myrtle, has been the selfish catalyst for both Myrtle and Gatsby's deaths. And Nick, who is so shocked and disappointed by the corrupt world he encounters in the East, is defeated and returns to his childhood home. There is no sense in *The Great Gatsby* of sentimentality being anything other than a dangerous illusion, and nostalgia is ultimately condemned as a futile indulgence.

BIBLIOGRAPHY

Edition used for this study guide:

Fitzgerald, F. Scott: *The Great Gatsby*, ed. Susanne Lenz. Stuttgart: Reclam, 1995 (reclams Universal Bibliothek Nr. 9242).

Other editions:

Fitzgerald, F. Scott: *The Great Gatsby*, introduction by Tony Tanner. London: Penguin, 2012 (Penguin Modern Classics). → Of the many paperback editions of *The Great Gatsby* available from British and American publishers, this is one of the few to include a scholarly introduction and notes on the text.

Secondary literature:

Bruccoli, Matthew Joseph: *Some Sort of Epic Grandeur: The Life of F. Scott Fitzgerald (Revised edition)*. Columbia, SC: University of South Carolina Press, 2002. → The standard Fitzgerald biography by the most important Fitzgerald scholar. An interesting read, providing much background detail and context for an understanding of the writer's work.

Prigozy, Ruth: *The Cambridge Companion to F. Scott Fitzgerald*. Cambridge: Cambridge University Press, 1997. → In-depth studies of Fitzgerald's writing for university students. An excellent but demanding source.

Film adaptations:

The Great Gatsby

1926 and 1949 → Two early versions, both of which are now lost: the 1926 version was a silent movie.

The Great Gatsby
USA1974.
Screenplay: Francis Ford Coppola. Director: Jack Clayton → Popular and well-liked adaptation with an excellent script and great casting, especially with Robert Redford as Gatsby and Bruce Dern as Tom, which suffers from being overly sentimental and which lacks much of the irony and commentary of the novel.

G.
USA 2002
Screenplay: Andrew Lauren. Director: Christopher Scott Cherot → Swiftly-forgotten modernised adaptation set in the world of hip hop, with Gatsby as an aspiring rapper who is rejected by a wealthy young woman and spends ten years building a hip hop empire.

The Great Gatsby
2013
Screenplay: Baz Luhrmann & Craig Pearce. Director: Baz Luhrmann → Starring Leonardo DiCaprio as Gatsby, and directed by the exciting and innovative Baz Luhrmann (Strictly Ballroom, 1992; Romeo + Juliet, 1996; Moulin Rouge, 2001), this film has been very successful, but has also been criticised for simplifying the novel.

Internet sources

http://greatgatsby.org/ → A new website, this includes links to interesting and useful PDFs of essays about the novel and its themes in the Resources section.

http://fitzgerald.narod.ru/crackup/056e-eho.htm → The text of Fitzgerald's essay *Echoes of the Jazz Age*.

INDEX

DIGITALES ZUSATZMATERIAL

Literarisch vernetzt! Über 600 Materialien online.

Neuerscheinungen, Aktionen, kostenlose Angebote und Infos rund um Literatur.

Melden Sie sich gleich an – es lohnt sich!*

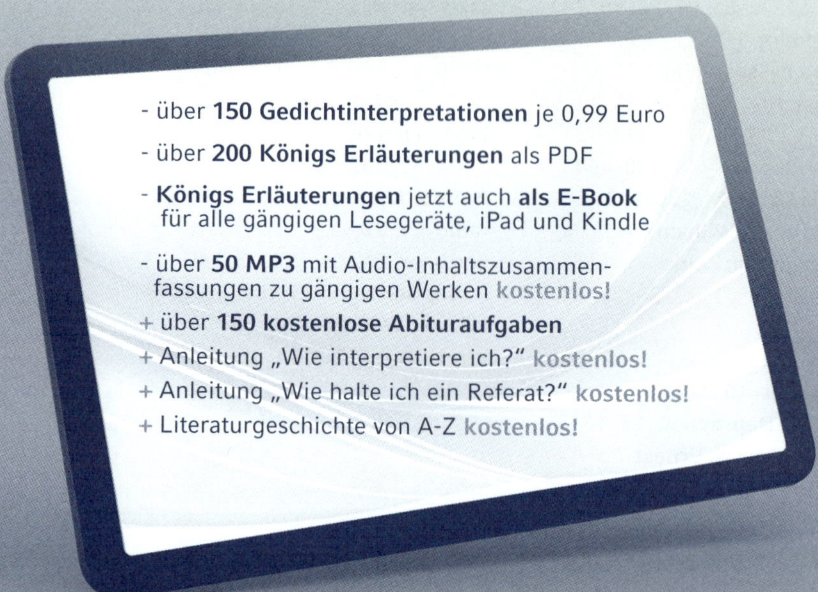

Seien Sie immer aktuell informiert mit unserem **Newsletter** oder über unsere **Social-media-Plattformen.**

Königs Erläuterungen

www.bange-verlag.de

* Sie erhalten max. 1 Newsletter monatlich!

facebook

www.königserläuterungen.de www.bange-verlag.de

KÖNIGS ERLÄUTERUNGEN
SPEZIAL

Alles zur Vorbereitung auf das Englisch-Abitur

→ wichtige Prüfungsthemen in allen Bundesländern
→ ideal zur Vorbereitung

My Son the Fanatic.
Textanalyse und Interpretation

- Hanif Kureishi: Leben und Werk
- Inhaltsangabe
- Aufbau
- Personenkonstellation und Charakteristiken
- Interpretationsansätze
- Rezeptionsgeschichte

Als E-Book

Shakespeare
bei den Königs Erläuterungen

- Hamlet
- Macbeth
- Much Ado About Nothing – Viel Lärm um Nichts
- Othello
- Romeo and Juliet – Romeo und Julia
- The Merchant of Venice – Der Kaufmann von Venedig

Als E-Book

Bange Verlag

Alles zur Vorbereitung auf Referat, Klausur, Abitur, und Matura
www.königserläuterungen.de

www.bange-shop.de

KÖNIGS ERLÄUTERUNGEN
SPEZIAL

Alles zur Vorbereitung auf das Englisch-Abitur

- wichtige Prüfungsthemen in allen Bundesländern
- ideal zur Vorbereitung

How to Cope with Statistics

Study and writing aids
for advanced learners

Dieser Kompaktkurs in Statistik für Einsteiger hilft beim Umgang mit Daten und Zahlen ebenso wie mit Tabellen und Diagrammen.

Als E-Book

**English Composition,
Focus on Commenting (AFB III)**

...a user-friendly primer of essential writing skills; suitable for classroom lessons and for self-teaching

Dieser Kompaktkurs macht Oberstufenschüler und Studenten mit den grundlegenden Anforderungen des Comments im Englischen vertraut.

Als E-Book

Bange Verlag

Alles zur Vorbereitung auf Referat, Klausur, Abitur und Matura
www.königserläuterungen.de

www.bange-shop.de